Ding Yi

丁乙

Timothy Taylor

泰勒画廊

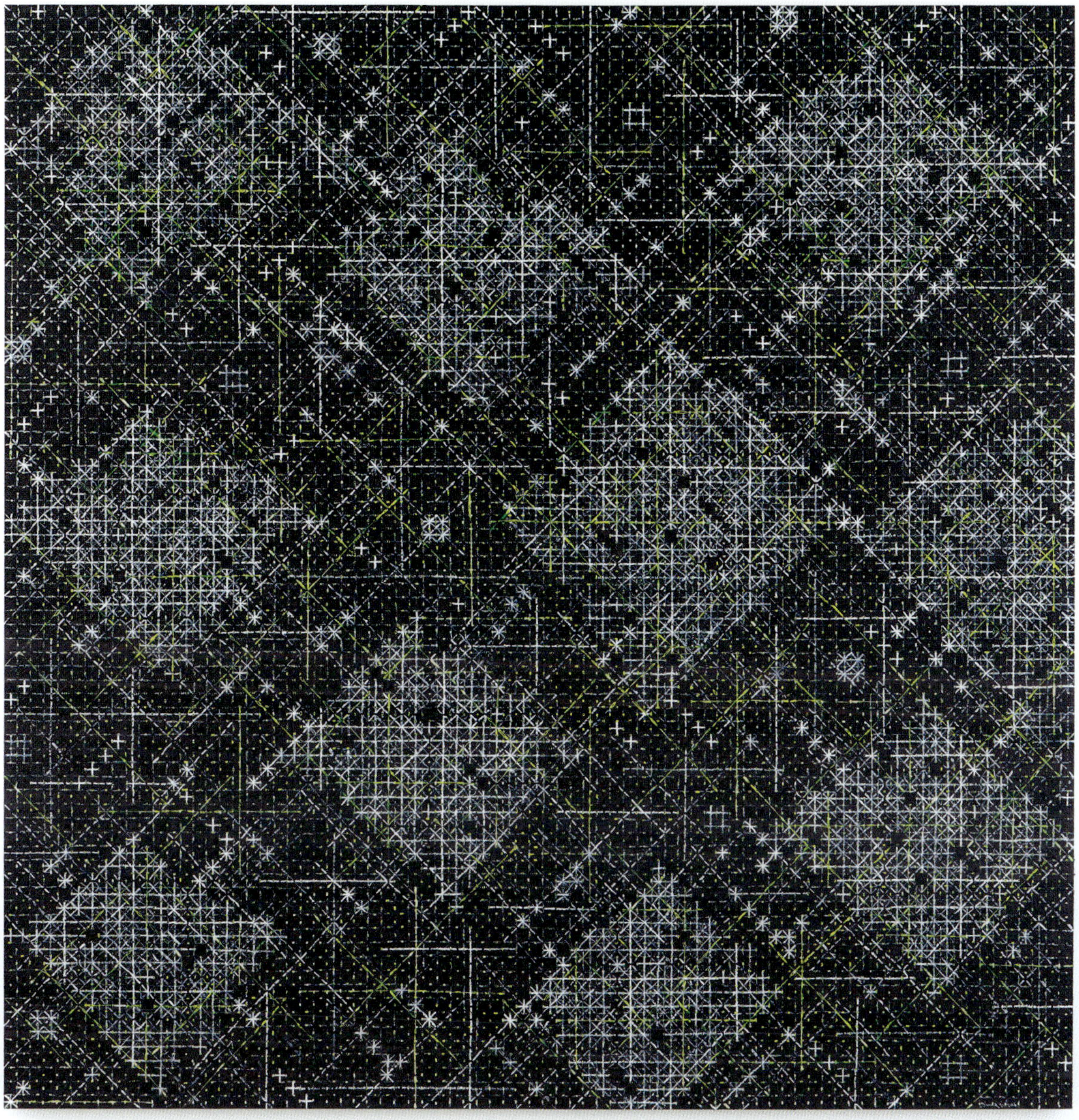

Appearance of Crosses 2016 - 4
(1:15 scale)

十示 2016 - 4
(1:15 比例尺)

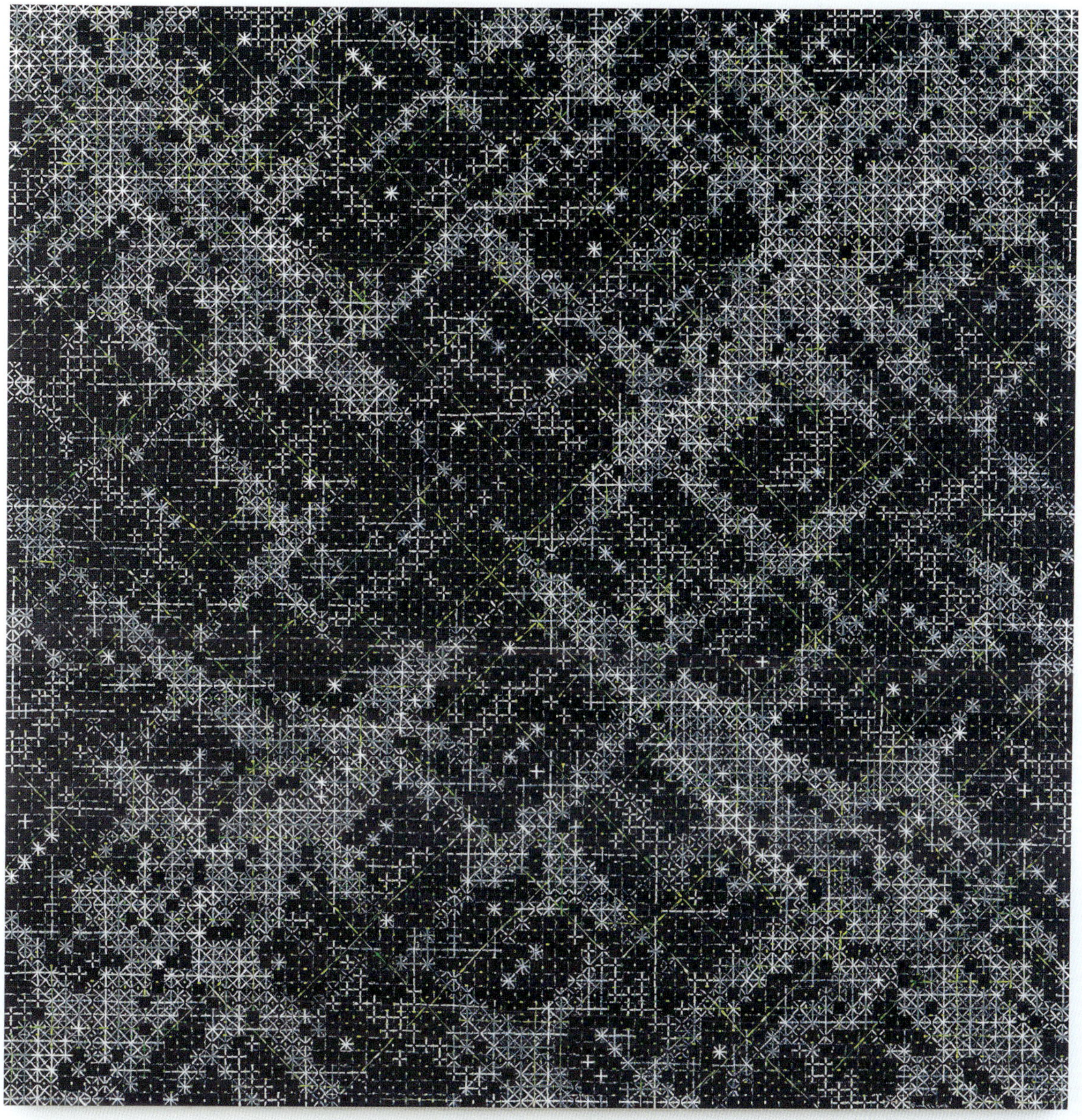

Appearance of Crosses 2016 - 5
(1:15 scale)

十示 2016 - 5
(1:15 比例尺)

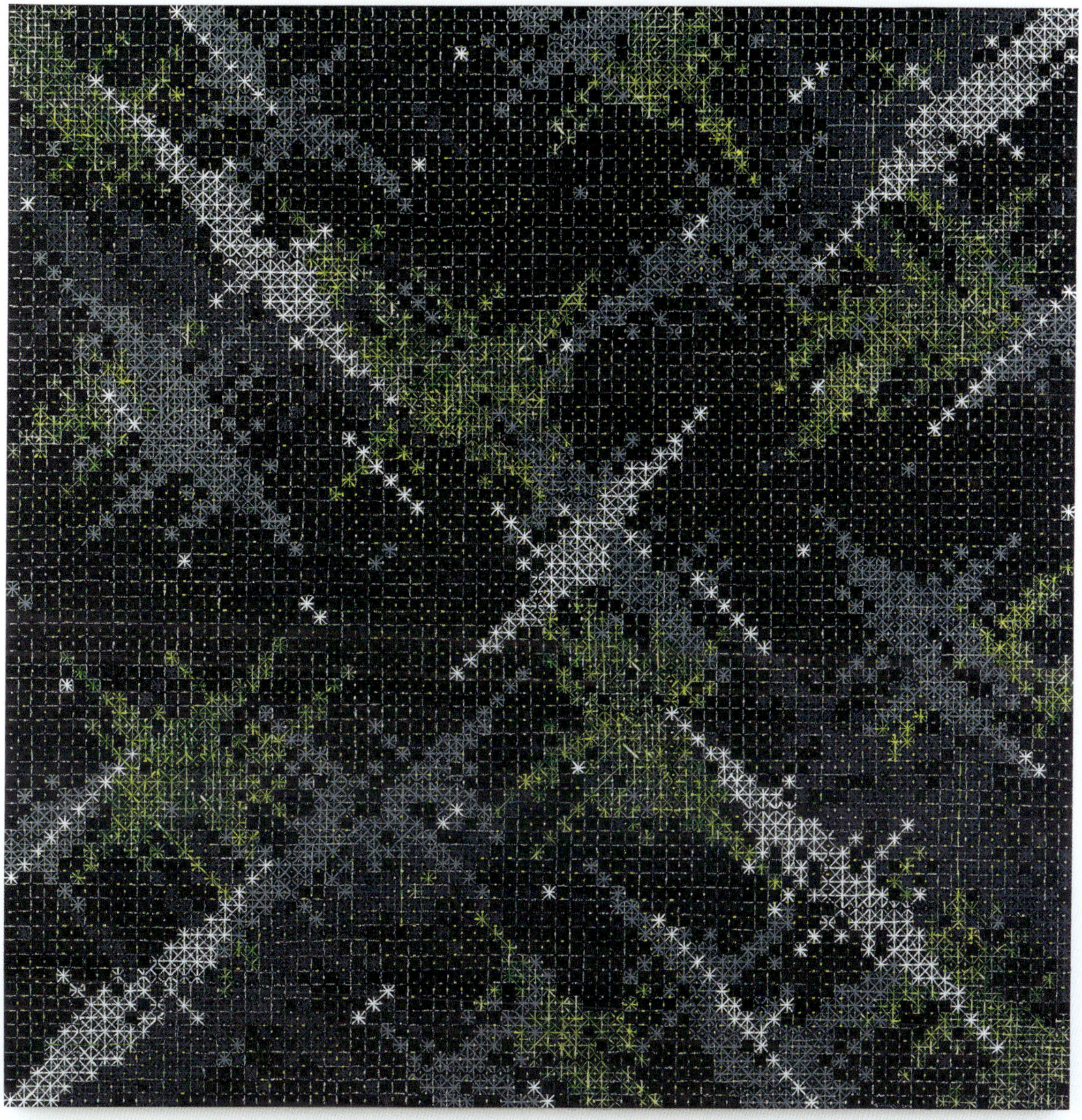

Appearance of Crosses 2016 - 6
(1:15 scale)

十示 2016 - 6
(1:15 比例尺)

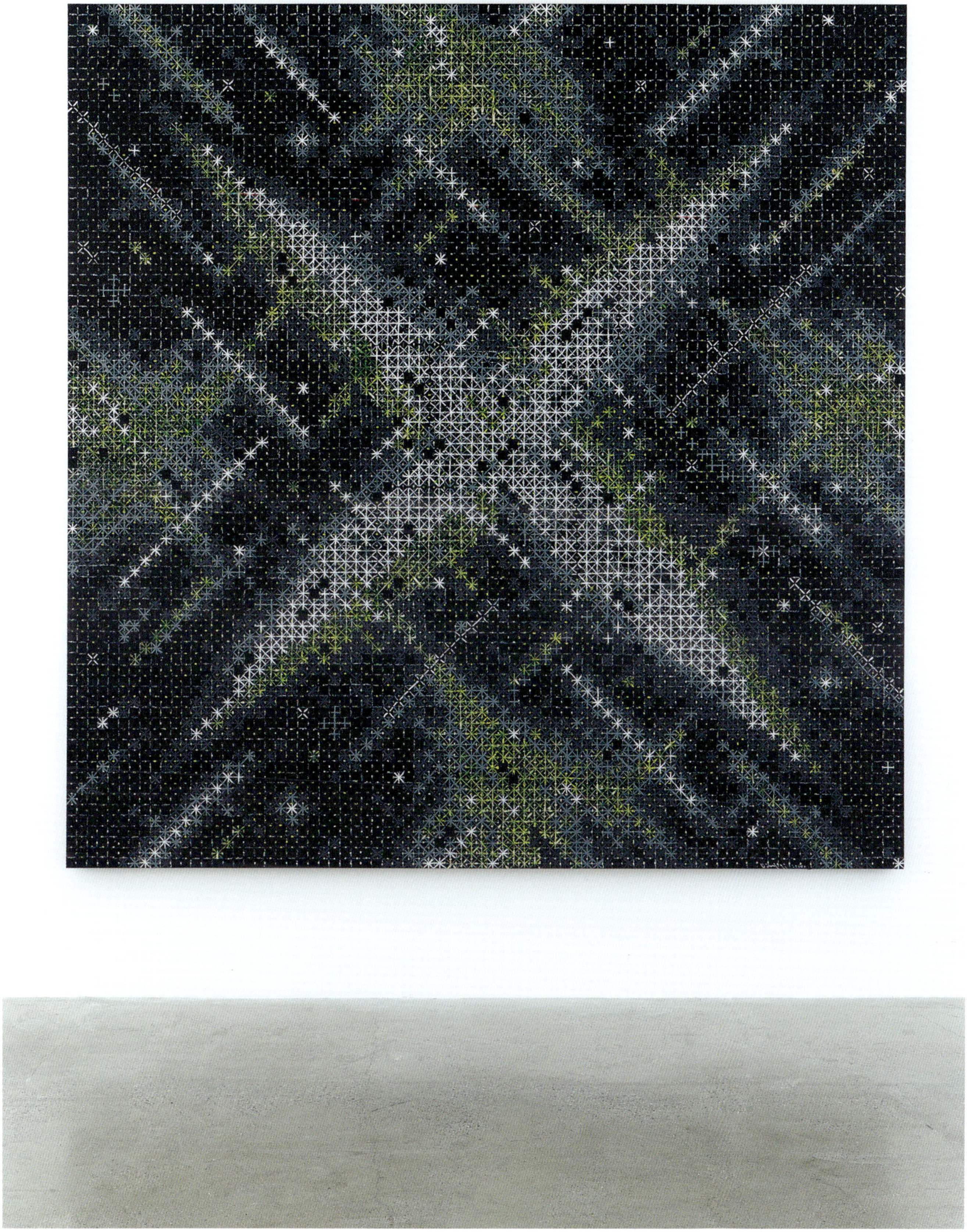

Appearance of Crosses 2016 - 7
(1:15 scale)

十示 2016 - 7
(1:15 比例尺)

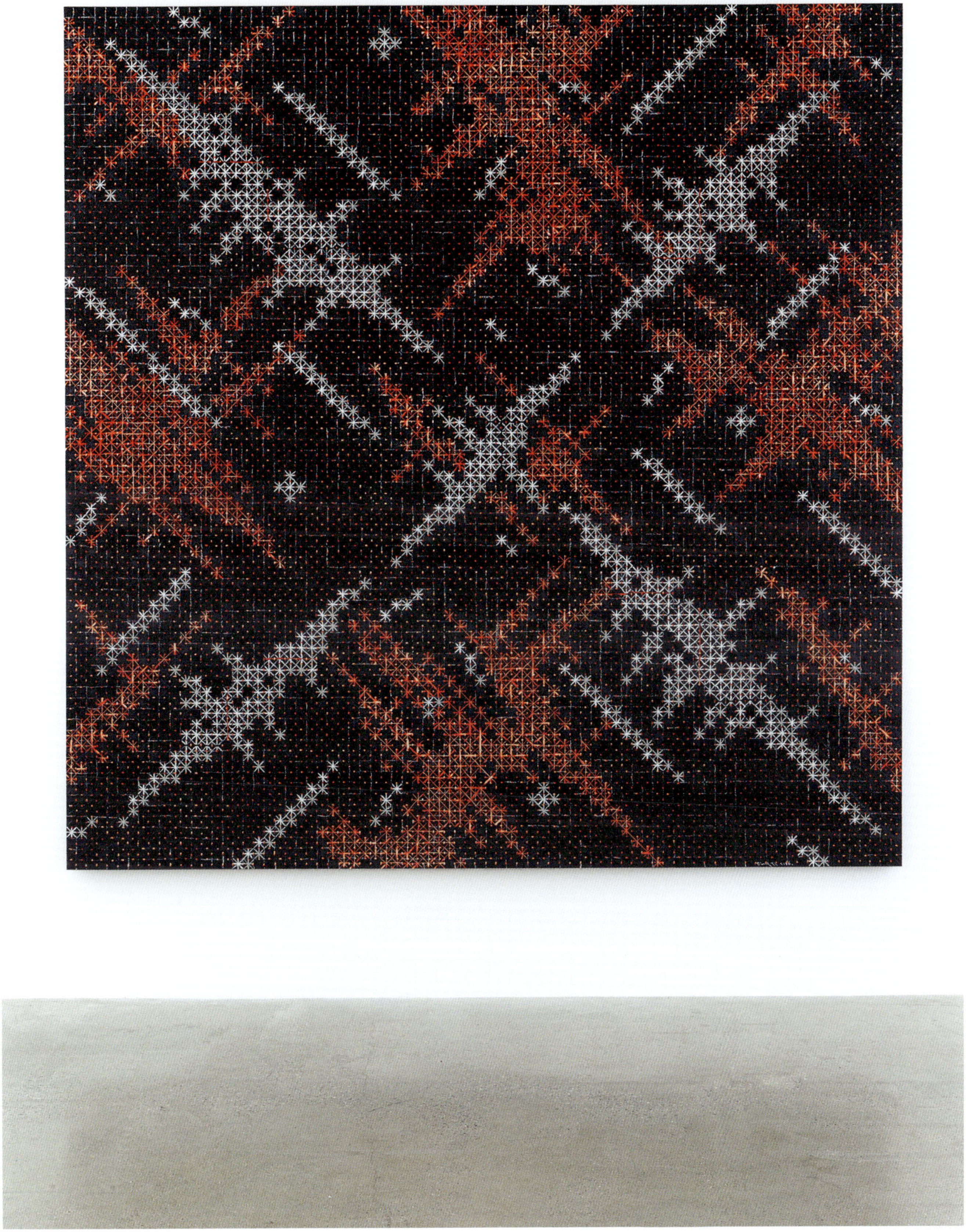

Appearance of Crosses 2016 - 8
(1:15 scale)

十示 2016 - 8
(1:15 比例尺)

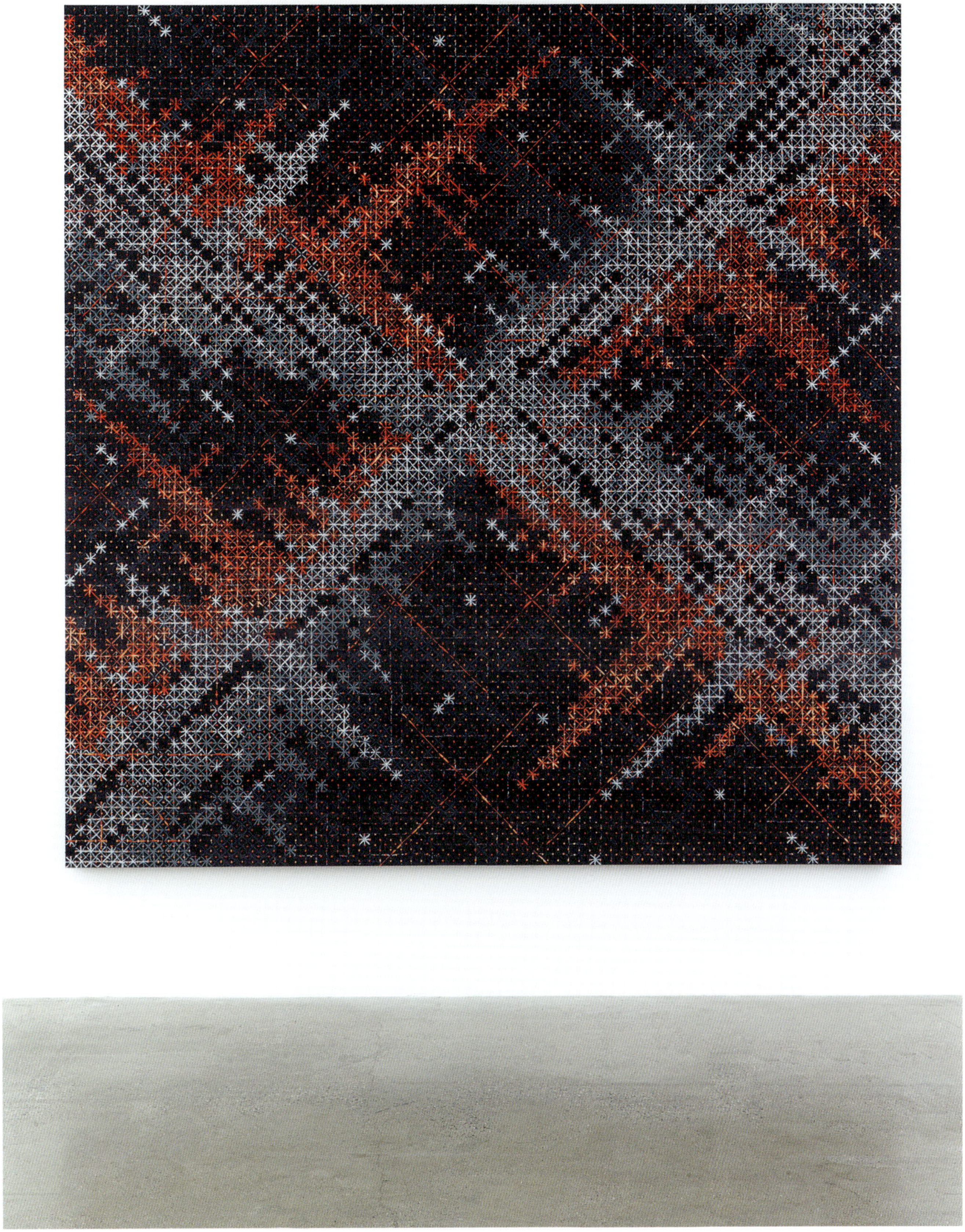

Appearance of Crosses 2016 - 9
(1:15 scale)

十示 2016 - 9
(1:15 比例尺)

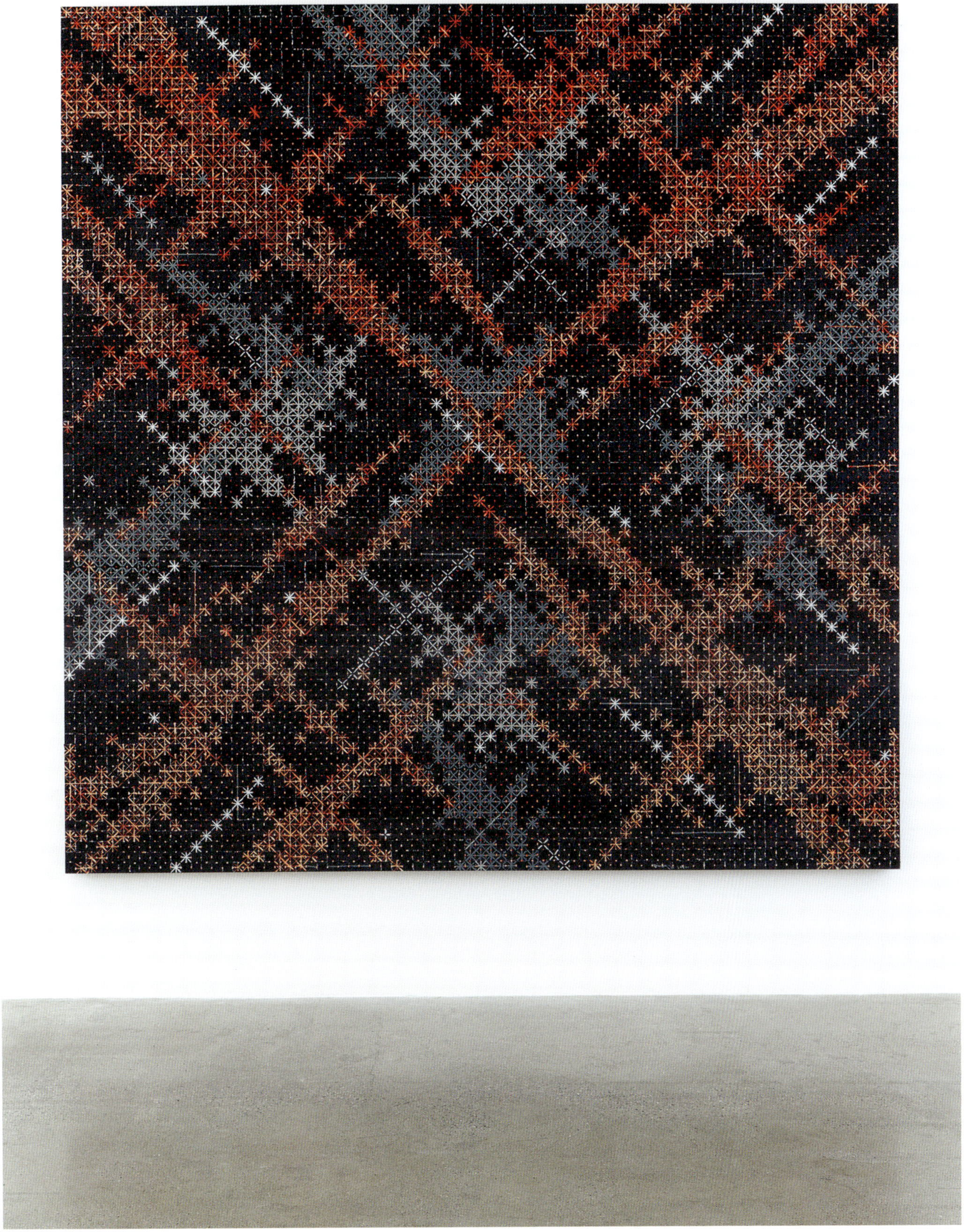

Appearance of Crosses 2016 - 10
(1:15 scale)

十示 2016 - 10
(1:15 比例尺)

All works
Mixed media on basswood
240 × 240 cm / 94 ½ × 94 ½ in

全部作品
椴木板上综合材料
240 × 240 cm / 94 ½ × 94 ½ in

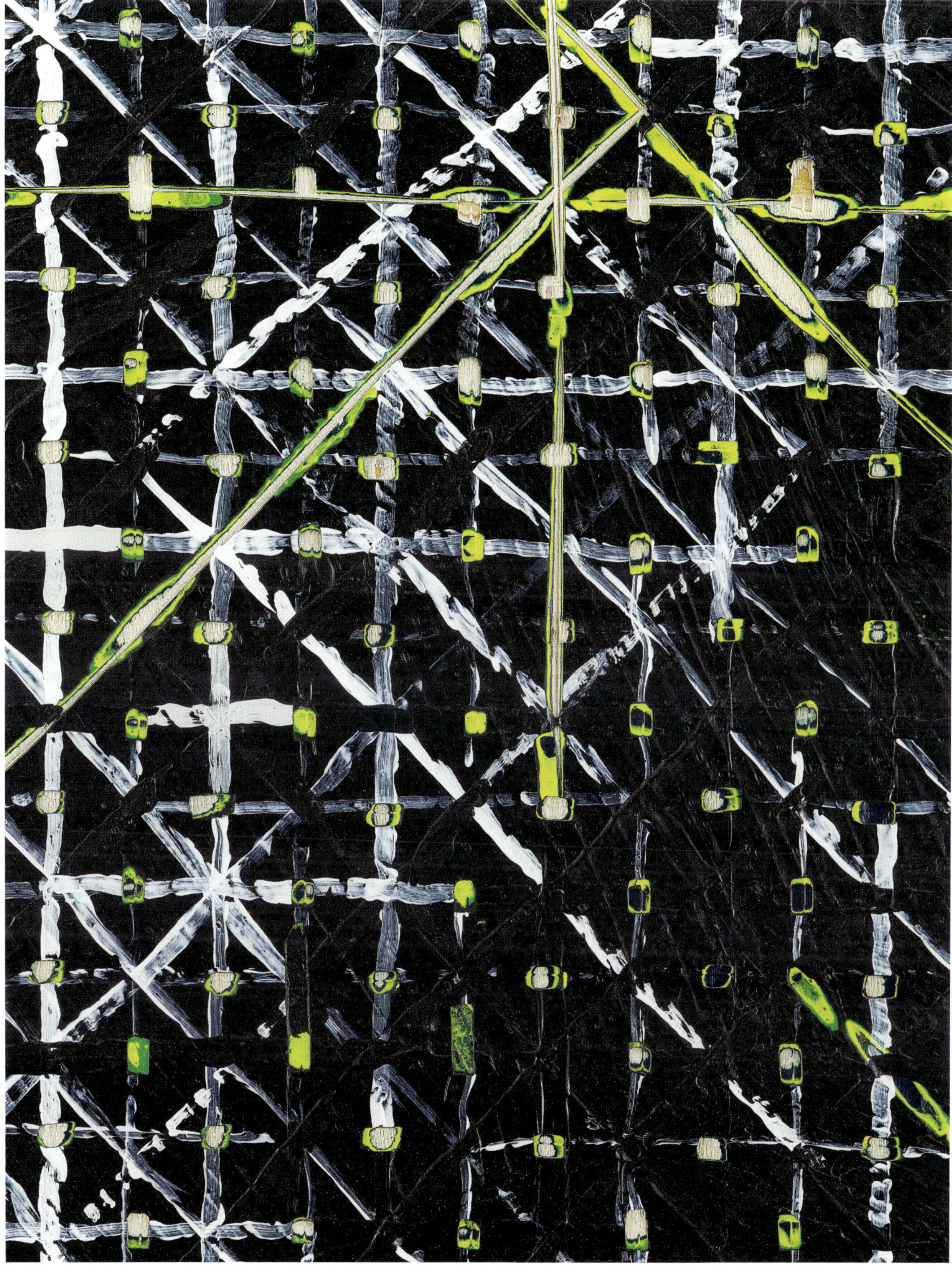

Appearance of Crosses 2016 - 4
(Detail, 1:1 scale)

十示 2016 - 4
(细节图，1:1 比例尺)

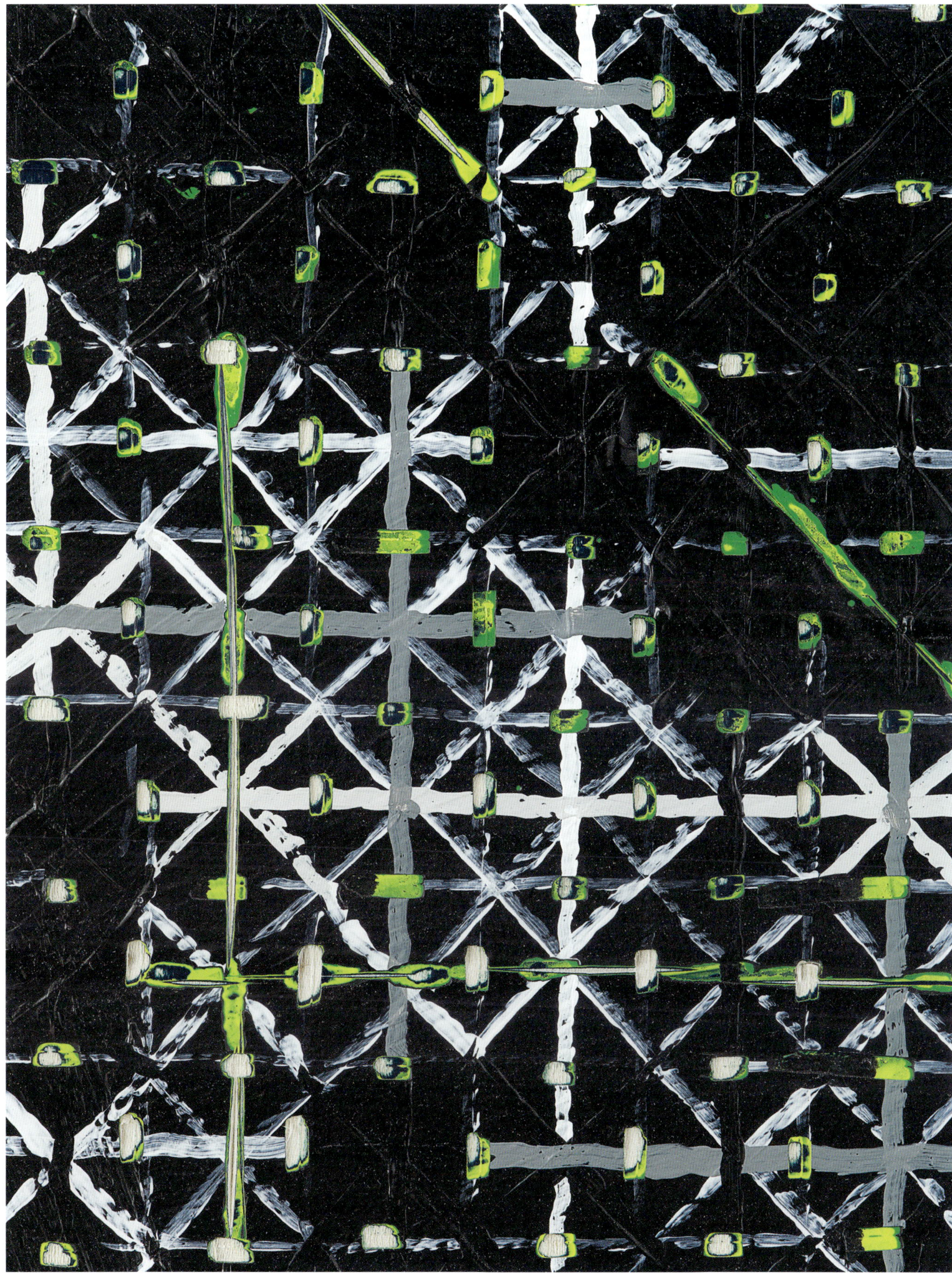

Appearance of Crosses 2016 - 5
(Detail, 1:1 scale)

十示 2016 - 5
(细节图，1:1 比例尺)

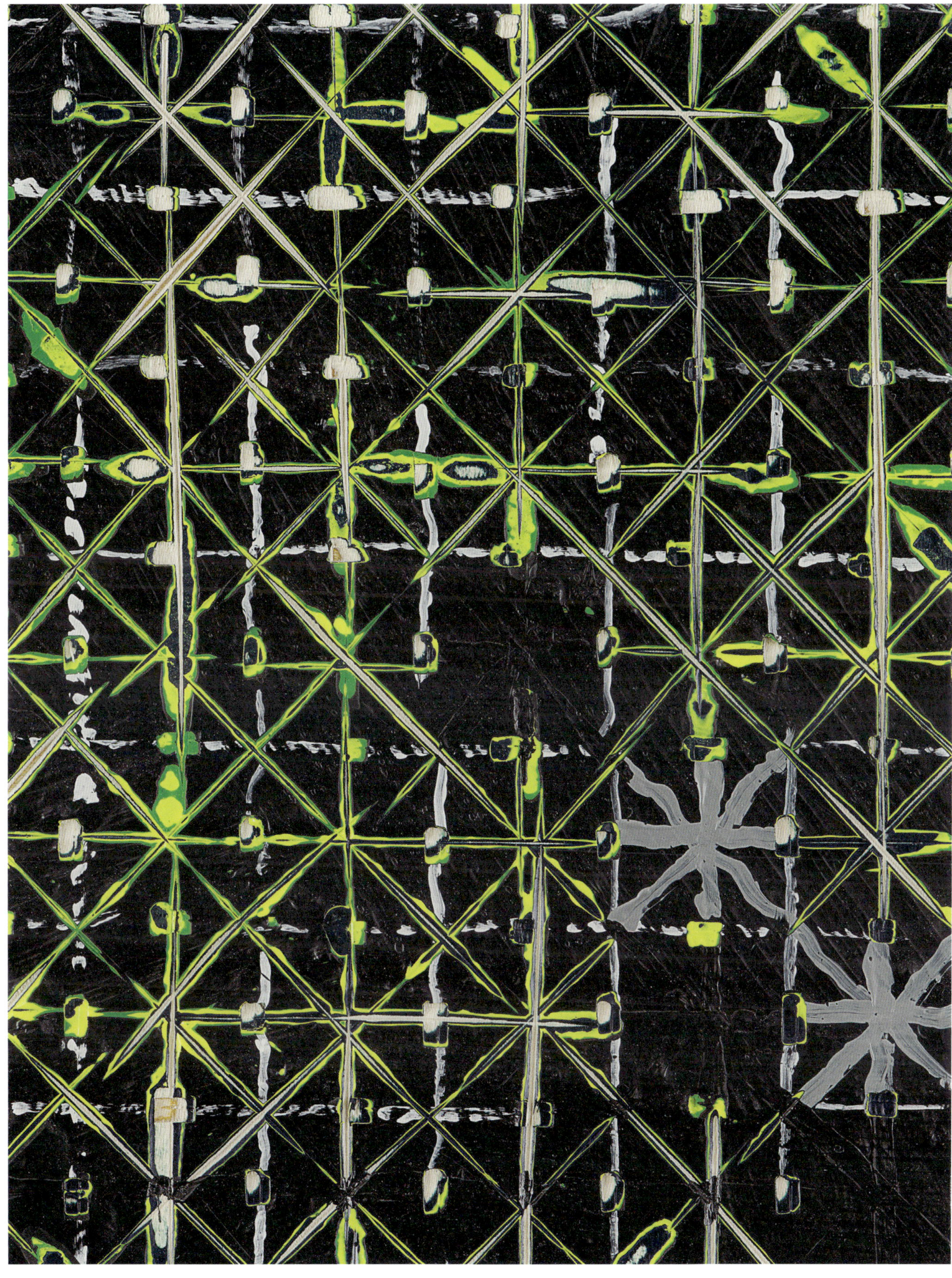

Appearance of Crosses 2016 - 6
(Detail, 1:1 scale)

十示 2016 - 6
(细节图，1:1 比例尺)

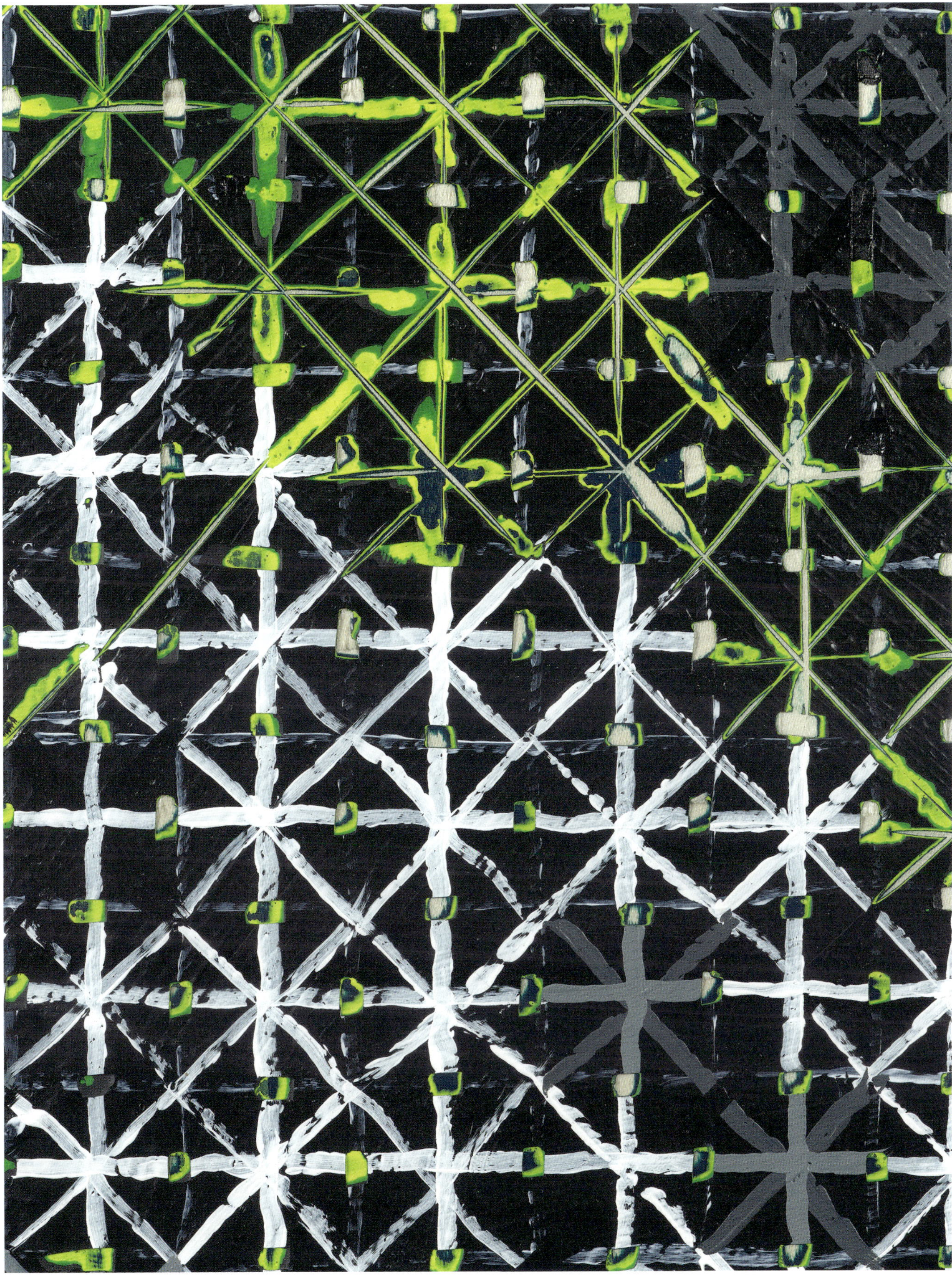

Appearance of Crosses 2016 - 7
(Detail, 1:1 scale)

十示 2016 - 7
(细节图，1:1 比例尺)

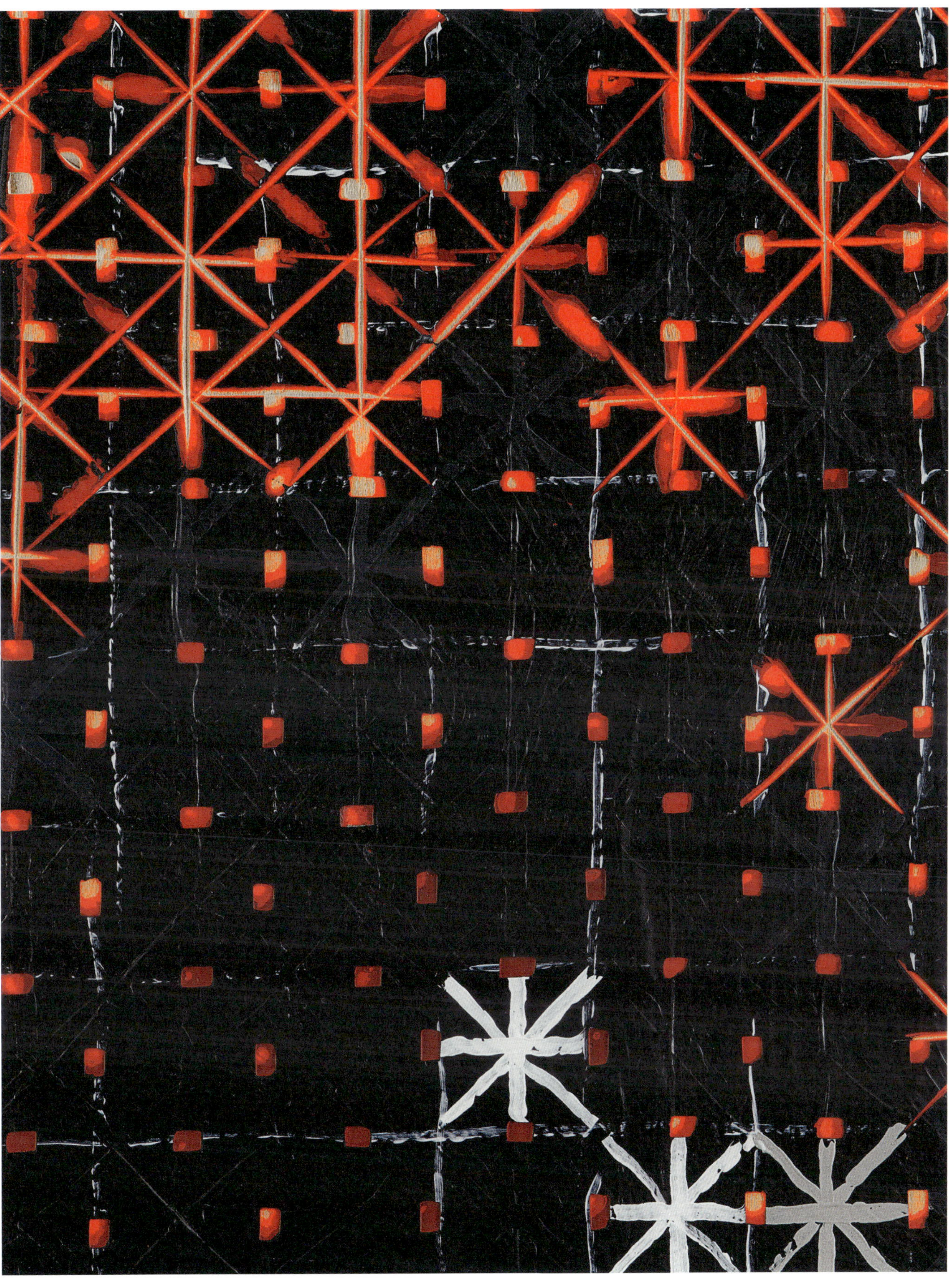

Appearance of Crosses 2016 - 8
(Detail, 1:1 scale)

十示 2016 - 8
(细节图，1:1 比例尺)

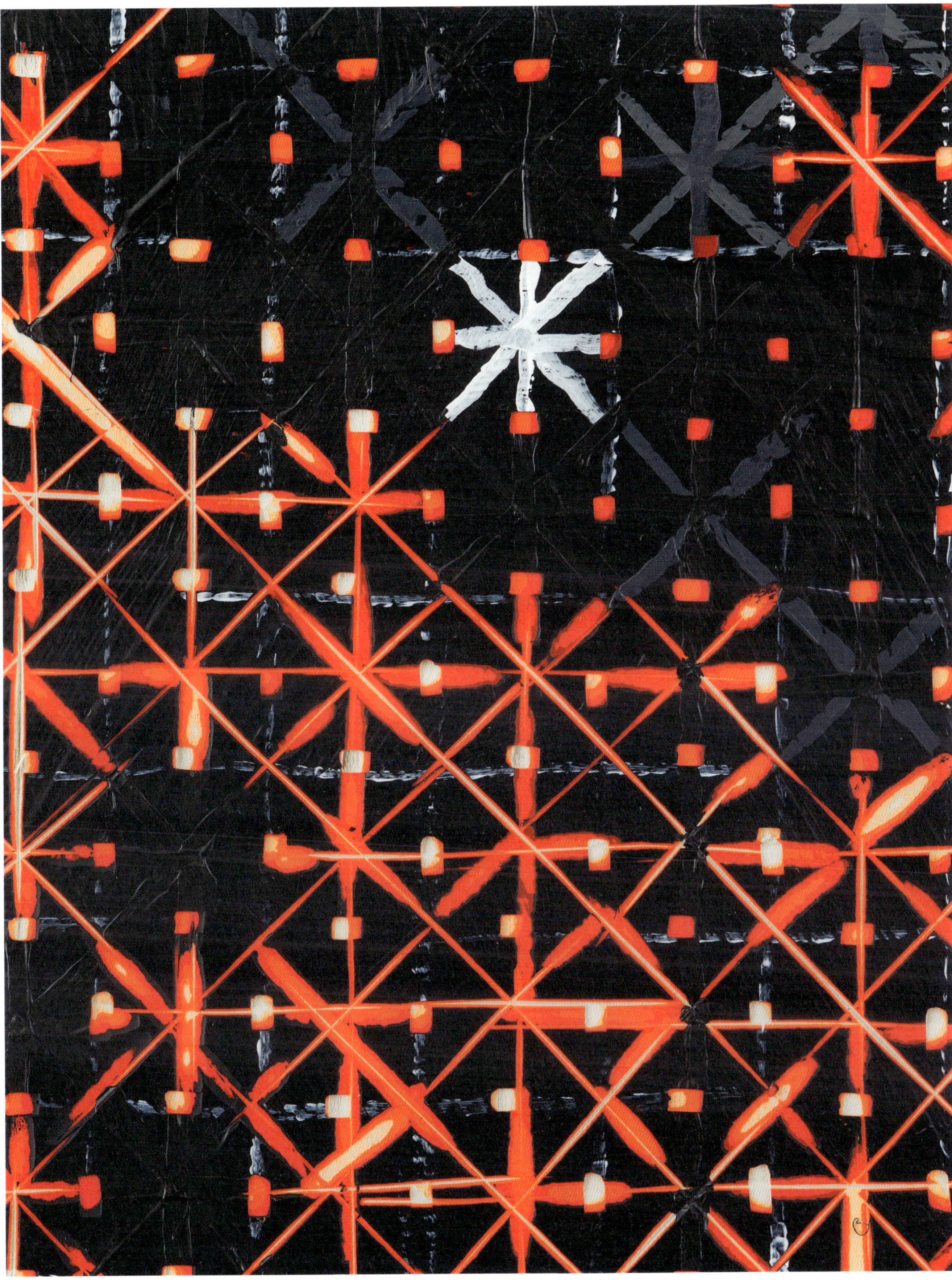

Appearance of Crosses 2016 - 9
(Detail, 1:1 scale)

十示 2016 - 9
(细节图，1:1 比例尺)

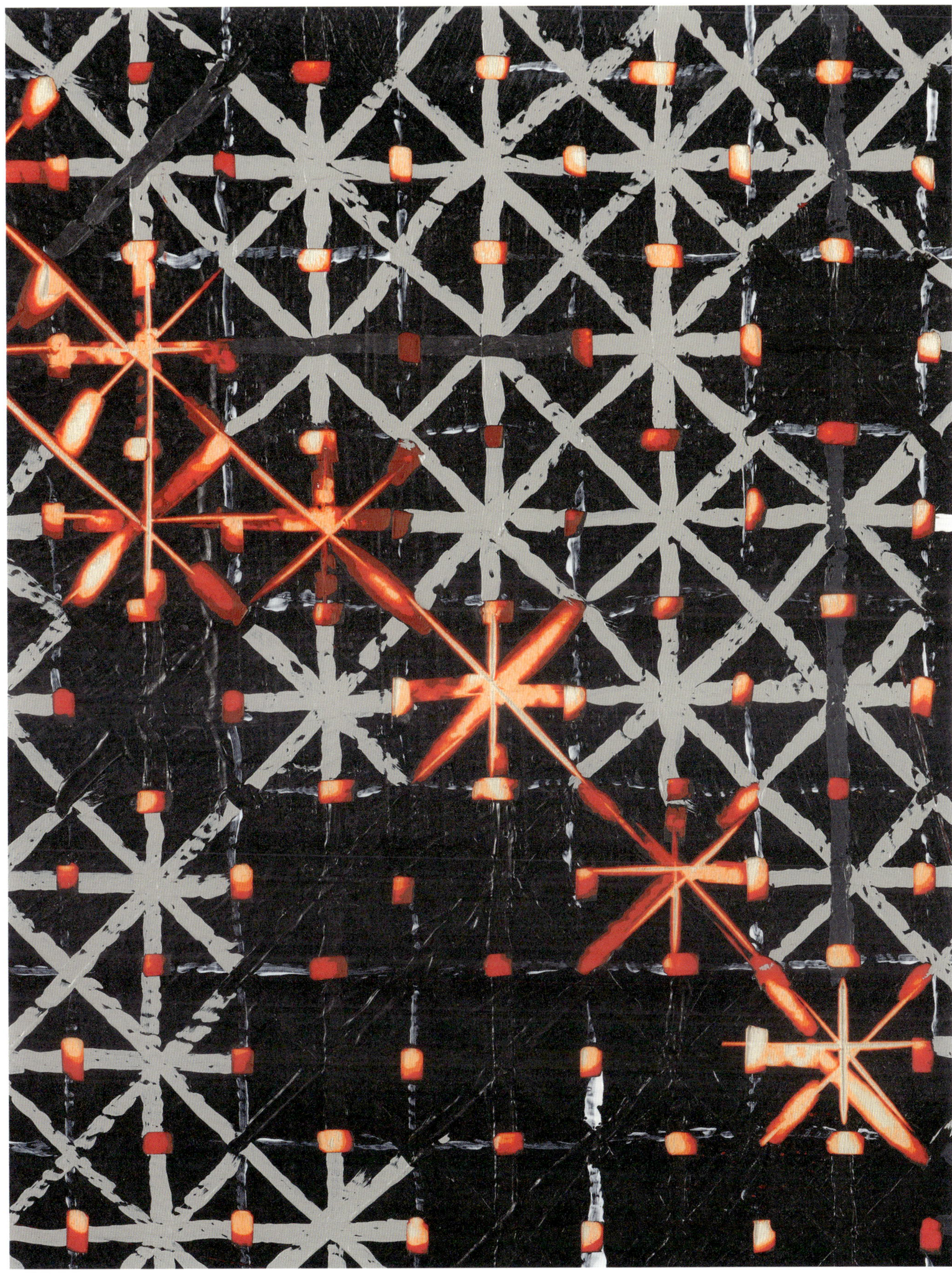

Appearance of Crosses 2016 - 10
(Detail, 1:1 scale)

十示 2016 - 10
(细节图，1:1 比例尺)

All works
Mixed media on basswood
240 × 240 cm / 94 ½ × 94 ½ in

全部作品
椴木板上综合材料
240 × 240 cm / 94 ½ × 94 ½ in

In September 2013, a small group of us walked into the Shanghai studio of China's foremost abstract painter, and I immediately felt at ease. I was full of anticipation for a filmed conversation that had been arranged to take place between Ding Yi and Sean Scully. Neither had met before and this was my first visit to a very new world. The studio was hidden in a warren of small lanes and I remember stepping up to enter the building. Ding Yi, there to greet us, could not have been more open, warm and welcoming, and had prepared a wonderful breakfast for his guests.
The meeting was both convivial and stimulating and from that moment I felt my first real excitement for China. This was the first of many meetings between these two great artists, who have since become close friends. It was the chance sighting by Ding Yi of one of Scully's early publications that brought our party to China and into Ding's studio.

Through the 1990s I followed the huge rise of interest in contemporary Chinese artists but never felt any context from which to truly understand these ambitious figures. As the years have passed, of course, having visited the country many times, things have increasingly fallen into place. This generation of artists has since looked beyond China with imagery and subject matter that has to an outsider often disguised, though still contained, the great traditional roots of Chinese philosophy and culture.

And it's from within traditional China, specifically the city of Shanghai, that I came to admire Ding Yi's paintings.
In a culture about which I knew very little at the time, I found myself asking many questions about the work of this remarkable contemporary artist from such a different world. What drew me to his paintings? Why were they so compelling? Was it the physicality, the palette, the surface or the absolute hand of the artist visible across every inch of these vast paintings? Standing before one of these large-format square works, I am confronted each time both with different answers and yet more questions – a feeling which always makes me smile. This paradox is why I love what I do. Compelling artists and works that challenge me always make the very best relationships and exhibitions, gradually revealing themselves as they evolve.

Ding Yi's paintings could not have been painted anywhere else, yet they transcend national boundaries. Graduating in the mid 1980s after training in the fine art of ink painting, Ding emerged as part of the avant-garde '85 New Wave movement – a generation of artists that includes Gu Dexin, Wang Guangyi, Xu Bing, and Zhang Peili. Now in his fifties, well-travelled and informed, through his thirty-year odyssey *Appearance of Crosses,* Ding and his works are well placed to absorb the rapid transformations under way in contemporary Chinese society.

It is with great pride that we are hosting Ding Yi's first exhibition in London and I would like to thank Hettie Judah and Martin Herbert for their considered texts. I must also thank Lorenz Helbling and ShanghART for their endorsement and for the generous support and friendship they have shown me over the years.
And, of course, Ding Yi, whose straightforward trust and faith in my gallery is the reason this great exhibition is possible.

Timothy Taylor

2013年9月，我们一行数人参观了中国首屈一指的抽象画家丁乙的上海工作室。一进入画室，我就觉得十分自在。此行是去拍摄丁乙和肖恩·斯库利(Sean Scully)的对谈，我对此充满期待。两位艺术家第一次见面，这也是我第一次去中国这个全新的世界。我记得，我们走入深藏在弄堂里的这间工作室，迎接我们的丁乙特别坦诚、热情和周到，为我们准备了丰盛的早餐。这次会面非常友好，让我获益良多。直到那时，我才开始对中国真正感到激动。两位伟大的艺术家之后又见了好几次，已经成为了好朋友。丁乙偶然看到过斯库利早期的一本画册，促成了我们的中国之行，并到访丁乙画室。

在1990年代的十年间，我注意到，各方对于中国当代艺术家的兴趣出现了大幅增加。但是，我缺乏相关背景，无法真正理解这些抱负不凡的人物。随着时间的推移，我去了中国几次，才逐渐有了更清楚的认识。近年来，这一代中国艺术家的图像和主题已经超越了中国。从局外人的视角看，他们的作品经常掩盖了中国传统哲学和文化的根基(虽然作品中仍然包含这种根基)。

正是从传统中国的角度，在上海这座城市里，我开始欣赏丁乙的作品。当时，我对中国文化知之甚少。丁乙这位卓越的当代艺术家来自非常不同的世界。看到他的作品后，我有许多问题想问。作品中的什么吸引了我?为什么它们那么令人叹服?是因为画作的活力、色调或表面?还是因为这些巨大的画作的每一寸画布上都清晰可见的、完全手工的笔触?看着这些大尺寸画作中的任意一件，我都会有不同的答案，也会有更多的问题出现——这种感觉却总是让我会心一笑。这样的悖论感也是我钟爱自己工作的原因。出众的艺术家和作品能激励我，让我和他们建立最佳的关系，也能呈现出最出色的展览，在不断演进中逐渐展露出更多内容。

丁乙的画作只可能诞生在上海，但是它们也是无国界的。1980年代中期，在学习了中国画之后，丁乙成为前卫的“85新潮”运动的一员(参加运动的艺术家还包括顾德新、王广义、徐冰和张培力)。他已经过了知命之年，见多识广。通过三十年来持之以恒地创作“十示”系列，丁乙和他的作品完美的体现了当代中国社会的迅速变革。

我们能举办此次丁乙伦敦的首展，倍感荣幸。我要感谢海蒂·朱达(Hettie Judah)和马丁·赫伯特(Martin Herbert)精心撰写的评论文章。我也要感谢何浦林(Lorenz Helbling)和香格纳画廊(ShanghART)对展览的支持，感谢他们过去几年里的鼎力帮助和情谊。最后，我要感谢丁乙，感谢他对我和画廊的信任，使得本次展览得以呈现他的杰作。

Timothy Taylor

Ding Yi: Towards a New Dynamism
Hettie Judah

丁乙:走向新动态
海蒂·朱达

There's a sense of acceleration within Ding Yi's recent works. Not in the speed of their creation – the loose-lined 'x' and '+' components from which these vast picture planes are constructed are all the fruit of meditative hand application – but in the scorching bright cut marks that slice through the layers of paint and etch into the supporting wood. Against the oily, inky black of the paintings' ground, the stark brightness of these exposed lines of wood and their attendant layers of fluorescent paint perform like superhighways for the eye, leading the gaze to zip along from one point to another.

Following a number of earlier series painted and drawn onto unexpected supports such as corrugated cardboard, unsized canvas, furniture, and, since 1997, prefabricated tartan, in this exhibition – the artist's first with Timothy Taylor – Ding Yi presents seven major new works each made on basswood. Ding's first large works on wood were created as a visual riposte to the gallery spaces at the Long Museum in Shanghai, site of his mid-career retrospective in 2015. 'There is an extremely tall space in the museum, which is over nine metres high, and the grey-coloured cement walls create an atmosphere that is cold and hard. Canvas was not able to show the strengths of the paintings in such a space, so I thought about using wood boards instead to conquer the space.'[1]

While chosen for its atmospheric, physical impact, in offering the possibility of a carved, almost sculptural aspect, wood has opened up a new field of exploration,

丁乙的近作体现出一种加速感，虽然他的创作速度并没有变化。作品巨大的画面由"x"和"+"等符号松散排布而成。艺术家一笔一笔徒手完成全部作品，如同冥想。作品的速度感体现在十分明亮的刻痕上。刻刀划过多层颜料，刻入底部木板表面。在油墨般的黑色基底上，这些暴露在外的木线和周边的荧光色层像视觉高速公路，把观者的视线迅速从一点引到另外一点。

丁乙部分早期的系列作品画在不寻常的材质上，例如瓦楞纸板、无浆帆布、家具和（1997年之后）成品格子布。在这次展览中（他在Timothy Taylor画廊的首展），艺术家将展出七件画在椴木板上的重磅新作。他第一批大型木板作品为上海龙美术馆2015年的个人回顾展而作，是对展览空间的视觉回应。"展厅巨大，九米多高，混凝土墙体，冷而坚硬，仅仅使用画布还不能在这个空间中显示绘画的力度。后来想到了用木板作为材料，来控制空间的场域。"[1]

丁乙选择木板，是因为木质对氛围和实体的影响，能够呈现刻划（几乎是雕塑似）的效果。木板给他带来了新的探索领域，代表了创作的新纪元：这个重要的新阶段延续了他对于表面和视觉平面

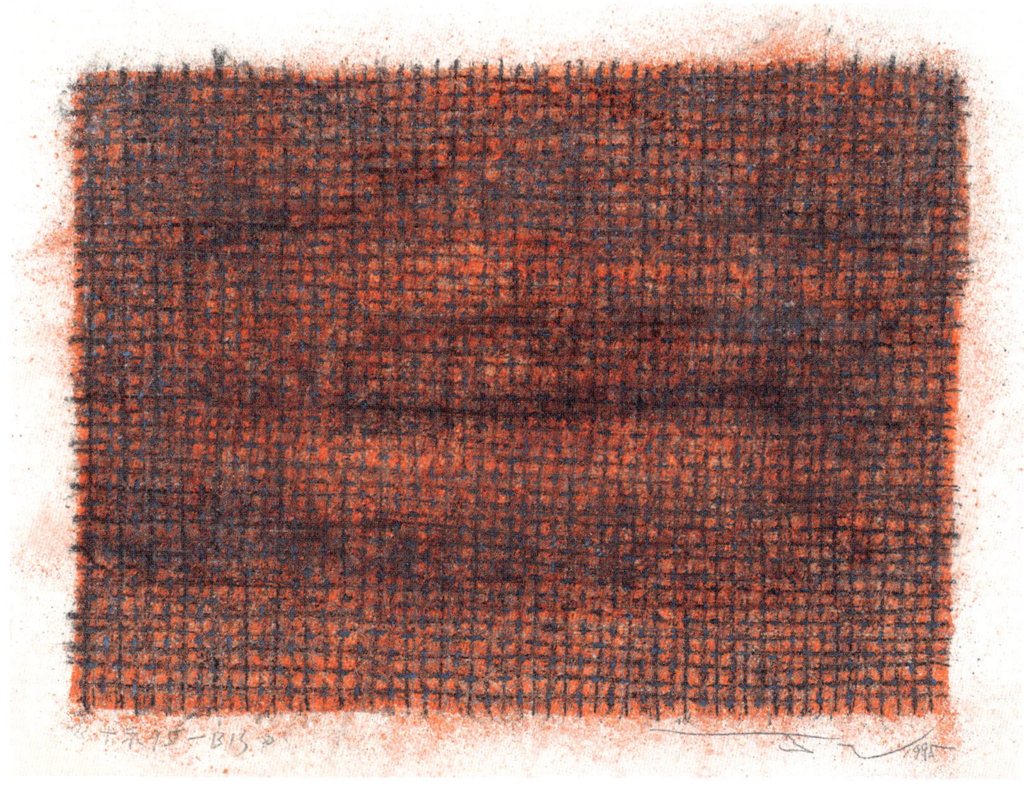

Appearance of Crosses 1995 - B13
(Scale 1:4)

十示 1995 - B13
(比例尺 1:4)

Appearance of Crosses 1995 - B21
(Scale 1:4)

十示 1995 - B21
(比例尺 1:4)

and with it, a new era in Ding's practice: one that marks a significant new phase of his ongoing exploration of the complex relationship between surface and optical planes, into what literally lies beneath. For where the crosses that Ding has worked with since the late 1980s usually perform as universal signifiers of combinative construction – the cement between bricks, a knot in two threads, plaited reeds, a road junction – these woodcut marks are more like excavations.

In this latest suite of works, Ding has built up layers of paint on the wooden surface – four works in yellow, green and black; three in orange, red and black – applied with a wide brush in varying thicknesses. In some – notably *Appearance of Crosses 2016 - 6* (see p. 5) – the base layers of paint are thick and uneven. The ridges of impasto in the black ground create a staccato effect in the white grid lines that are painted lightly across them: the laden paintbrush has skipped over the surface, touching only the crests of each underlying brushstroke. Beneath the dark surface, accretions of neon paint become sites of latent power – seething-hot colour waiting to be released by the slice of a woodblock cutter. 'I wanted to create an embryonic energy in these works rather than something that has grown and gone away,'[2] Ding has said.

This latency, this sense of forces waiting to be unleashed, is there too in the works' discreet referencing of cityscapes. While these are not paintings of places, they perform compellingly as dynamic, almost kinetic portraits of 'non-places': aerial, night-time snapshots of what Marc Augé terms the 'city world',[3] sliced up routes and boundaries, places of movement and human intermingling, all under bright and neon lights. Within each painting, the black layer, which Ding likens to 'a blackboard, or a blank stone tablet,'[4] occupies a position akin to that of the ground beneath our feet. Above the surface there is open space for construction; beneath it is a hidden world, like archaeological traces of a city, which can only be revealed and brought into conscious memory by breaking the surface. Ding's works have long suggested the passing of time and the bustle and motion of human life. Their regularly bright – and, since the early 2000s, often neon – colour palettes, and the relentless proliferation of cross markings across their surfaces have, in various series, recalled the shifting crowds and pulsing lights of the modern networked city. 'Though I am an abstract artist, in recent years I have started to take note of the urban development of Shanghai,'[5] he has said.

The geographer Yi-Fu Tuan draws explicit links between the innate human tendency for pattern recognition, the ability to visualise virtual concepts and the structuring of built environments: 'Human beings not only discern geometric patterns in nature and create abstract spaces in the mind, they also try to embody their feelings, images and thoughts in tangible material. The result is sculptural and architectural space, and on a large scale, the planned city'.[6]

之间复杂关系的长期研究，力图寻找平面之下隐藏的内容。1980年代末期以来，丁乙一直在使用十字符号。通常来说，这个符号的功能是结合性架构的普遍能指（universal signifiers），好似砖块之间的水泥、两根绳子打成的结、芦苇草编或是岔路口；新作品里的木刻则更像是考古挖掘的结果。

最近的系列作品中，丁乙在木质表面上堆积了数层颜料（其中四件作品的用色是黄、绿和黑；三件是橙、红和黑），宽阔的笔法涂出不同厚度的色层。在有些作品中——最明显的例子是《十示 2016-6》（见第5页），颜料基底厚重，高低起伏。黑色背景中，厚涂的隆起上轻轻地画了多条白色的网格线，产生了断奏曲的效果：饱蘸颜料的画笔跃过画面，只和隆起基底的顶部接触。在黑色的表面下，霓虹色颜料堆积的地方充满了潜在力量，火热的颜色亟待被木刻刀切开，得到释放。丁乙说："我想在这批作品中塑造某种正在萌发的力量，而不是已经发散出去的。"[2]

这种潜伏状态和力量呼之欲出的感觉也体现在了作品对城市风景含蓄的参照中。这些画作不是描绘场所（places）的作品，但是它们是对"非场所"（non-places）充满活力的描摹，几乎呈现出动态状。它们像夜景鸟瞰图，反映出马克 · 奥吉（Marc Augé）笔下的"都市世界"（city world）。[3] 划开的道路和边界、移动的场所和混杂的人群全部展现在明亮的霓虹灯下。在这些作品中，黑色的表面被丁乙比作"一块黑板，或者是一块石碑"。[4] 其地位就像是我们脚下的大地。表面之上有可供建设的开放空间；表面之下则是一个隐藏的世界，仿佛一座城市的考古遗迹，只有打破表面才能显露出来，成为意识记忆（conscious memory）的一部分。一直以来，丁乙的作品都在暗示时间的流逝和人类生活的运动和喧嚣。在多个系列中，作品用色明亮（自从2000年代早期开始，艺术家经常使用霓虹色），表面的十字符号无尽扩散，让人想起现代网格化都市中形状不断变化的人群和脉动的灯光。他说过："虽然我是一个抽象艺术家，但是近些年我开始关注上海的城市发展。"[5]

地理学家段义孚认为，人类天生的模式识别能力、虚拟概念视觉化的能力和建筑环境的结构性之间有着清晰的关联。"人类不光可以辨识自然界的几何图形，在大脑里构建抽象空间，也能够用可见的材料体现情感、图像和思维。最终能建成雕塑性和建筑性的空间以及（在一个宏

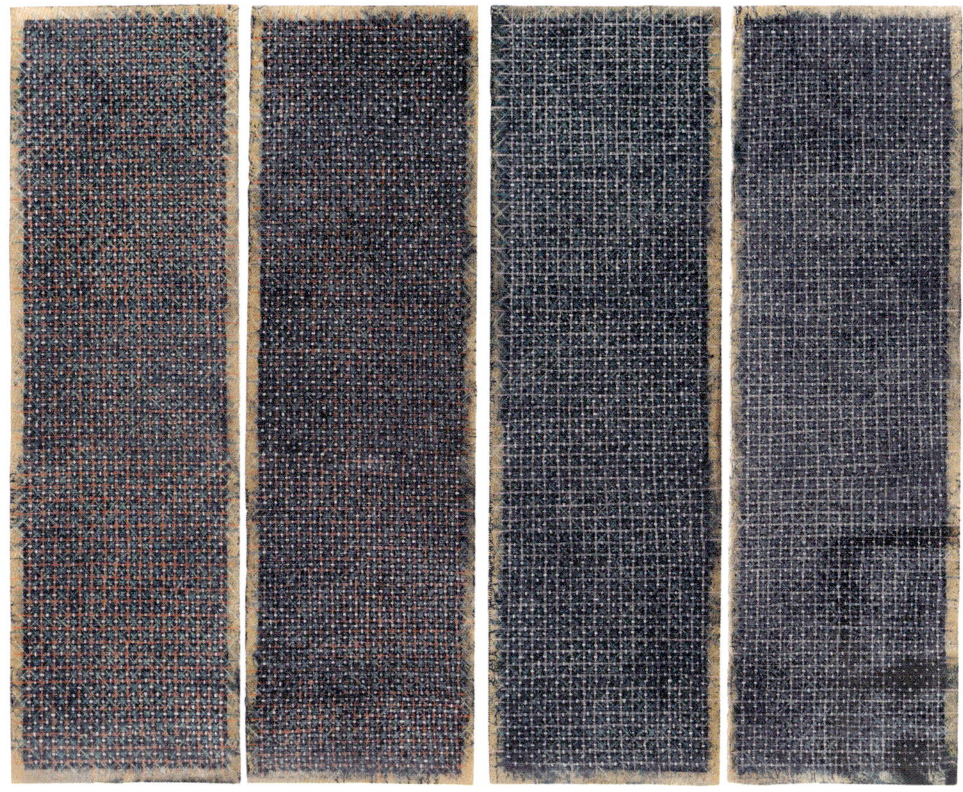

Appearance of Crosses 1997-B21 – 1997-B24
(Scale 1:24)

十示 1997-B21 – 1997-B24
(比例尺 1:24)

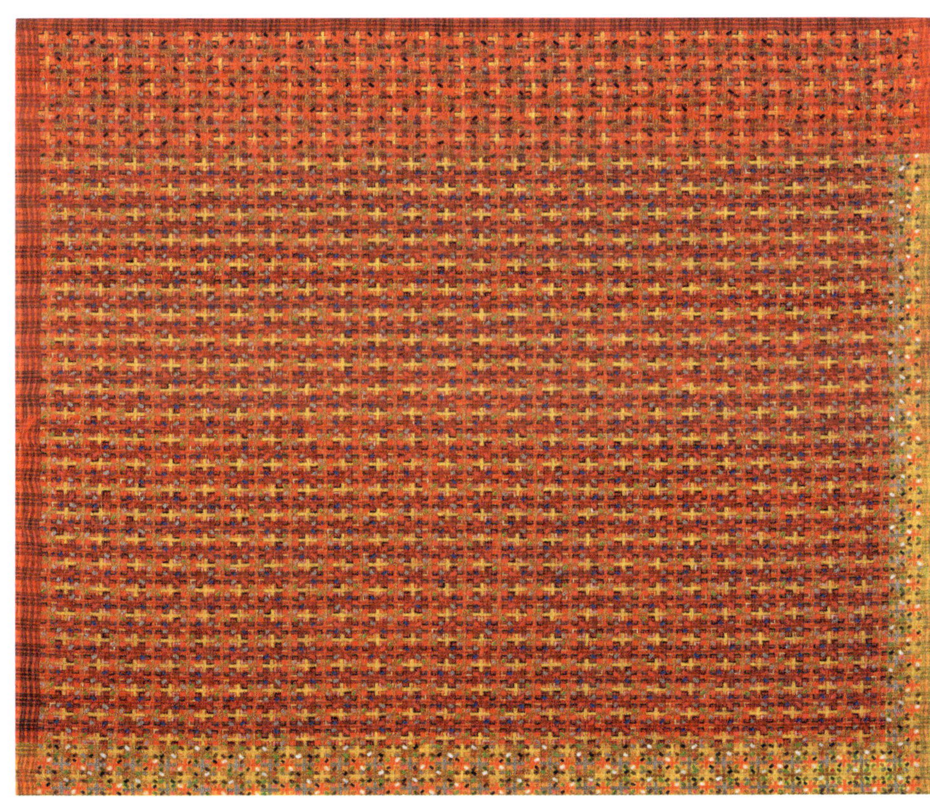

Appearance of Crosses 2000-8
(Scale 1:10)

十示 2000-8
(比例尺 1:10)

Ding Yi's *Appearance of Crosses 2016-4–2016-10* (see pp. 1–29) evoke all these elements of intellectual and sensory perception: the city, virtual space, networks of human relationships, but perhaps above all the desire of the roving eye to attribute logic and order to otherwise abstract and enigmatic arrangements of shapes and patterns.

Ding Yi is fascinated by design and pattern in their broadest and deepest senses. This is not something that the artist undertakes with an untutored eye: 'Because I majored in design at the Shanghai Arts and Crafts Institute, design was a constant influence for me, and I wanted to graft art and design together.'[7] The earliest *Appearance of Crosses* paintings borrowed from the visual languages of printing and graphic design: the cross itself was taken from a technical mark used in offset printing, and some of the first works were made using precision tools that would remove any possibility of a painterly effect.[8] The early design references in Ding's works had a subversive edge, gently undermining taboos in the avant-garde art world against craft and applied artforms.[9] His early experiments with texture, porosity and other variations in his painting surfaces produced a soft, worn effect in works such as *Appearance of Crosses 1997-B21–1997-B24* (see p. 37) that Cao Weijun has described as 'very much like an ancient textile just excavated from a tomb'.[10] Works on paper from this time – notably *Appearance of Crosses 1995-B13* and *1995-B21* (see p. 35) – recall samples of hand weaving:

大尺度之上的）经过规划的城市"。[6] 丁乙的《十示 2016-4》到《十示 2016-10》（见第1-29页）系列作品让人想到城市、虚拟空间和人类关系网络等智力和感观认知的元素。可能最重要的是，它们让观者看到，艺术家流动的视角在大量抽象和神秘的形状和样式中建立逻辑和秩序。

丁乙对于设计和样式十分着迷，研究力求深广。在这个领域，丁乙有着扎实的功底。他曾经说过："因为工艺美校的专业是设计，所以设计就一直影响我，要将绘画与设计进行嫁接。"[7] 最早的《十示》作品借鉴了印刷和平面设计的视觉语言。十字源自于平版印刷的十字标志。艺术家在早期的一些作品中使用了精确工具，在画布上消解掉所有可能留下的痕迹。[8] 这些作品中对设计的参考有颠覆的性质，轻巧地打破了当时前卫艺术圈对于工艺和实用艺术的禁忌。[9] 他尝试在不同质地、疏密和特性的表面上创作，产生出一种柔软的、做旧的作品效果。《十示1997-B21–1997-B24》（见第37页）就是一个例子。曹维君评价它"使人联想到[...]出土的织物"。[10]那段时间创作的纸上作品——最典型的是1995年的《十示 1995-B13》和《十示 1995-B21》（见第35页），像是手工编织的样本：层叠的网

the layered grids suggesting meshes of fine coloured threads, disintegrating into wisps of filament at the edges.

Ding's subsequent use of tartan cloth was, initially, less an engagement with another craft tradition than with a readymade set of grids and crosses: a base structure against which his 'single unit of grid' could build up 'like brushwork that combines to form the whole image'.[11] In *Appearance of Crosses 2000-8* (see p. 37) and *2000-9* (see opposite) the tartan is still visible as a faint ghost around the margins of Ding's painting, in which fields of shifting pattern and coloration demarcate planes, panes and zones.

The cultural depth in the use of tartan in Ding's practice is rooted in the long and complex history of trade between Scotland and China. In the second half of the nineteenth century, the enforced opening of the 'Treaty Ports' to Western trade made Shanghai and its surrounding region – long the lodestar for fashionable dress in greater China – the entry point for European textiles,[12] among them plaid. Traditional Scottish tartan was a rough woollen cloth, the colour of its yarn derived from locally available plant sources. Each region having subtly different vegetation, the colours of the tartan came to be directly associated with the people of that place. Much later specific woven patterns and colorations came to be formally associated with individual Scottish clans. Following an eighty-year period in which the wearing of tartan was banned in Scotland, in the 1820s the tartan industry was reborn. By the time the British established

格看似彩线织成的网，在边缘处解体成缕缕细线。

丁乙在接下来几年中使用苏格兰格子布作为画布。这个选择不是为了彰显格子布的手工艺传统，而是利用布面已有的网格和十字。在这个基本结构上，"一个单元符号"聚集在一起，"像是一种组织画面的一个笔触"。[11]在《十示 2000-8》（见第37页）和《十示 2000-9》（见右上图）中，丁乙绘画的边缘还能看见格子布的痕迹，像淡淡的幽灵。这些作品中，不断变化的样式和颜色界定出不同平面、方框和区域。

丁乙创作中使用格子布的文化深度来源于苏格兰和中国之间长期复杂的贸易史。十九世纪后半叶，被迫向西方贸易开放的"通商口岸"让格子布等欧洲纺织品通过上海和周边区域进入中国（该地区一直走在中国服装的最前沿）。[12] 传统苏格兰花格子布是结实的羊毛布料，纱线颜料提取自当地的植物。每个地区的植被都有些许不同，因此它们各自的格子布直接代表了这些地区的居民。经过长时间发展，每个苏格兰氏族的格子布都有了自己独特的样式和颜色。有八十年的时间里，苏格兰禁止穿格子布。禁令结束后，在1820年代，格子布产业得到了重生。约二十年之后，英国建立了

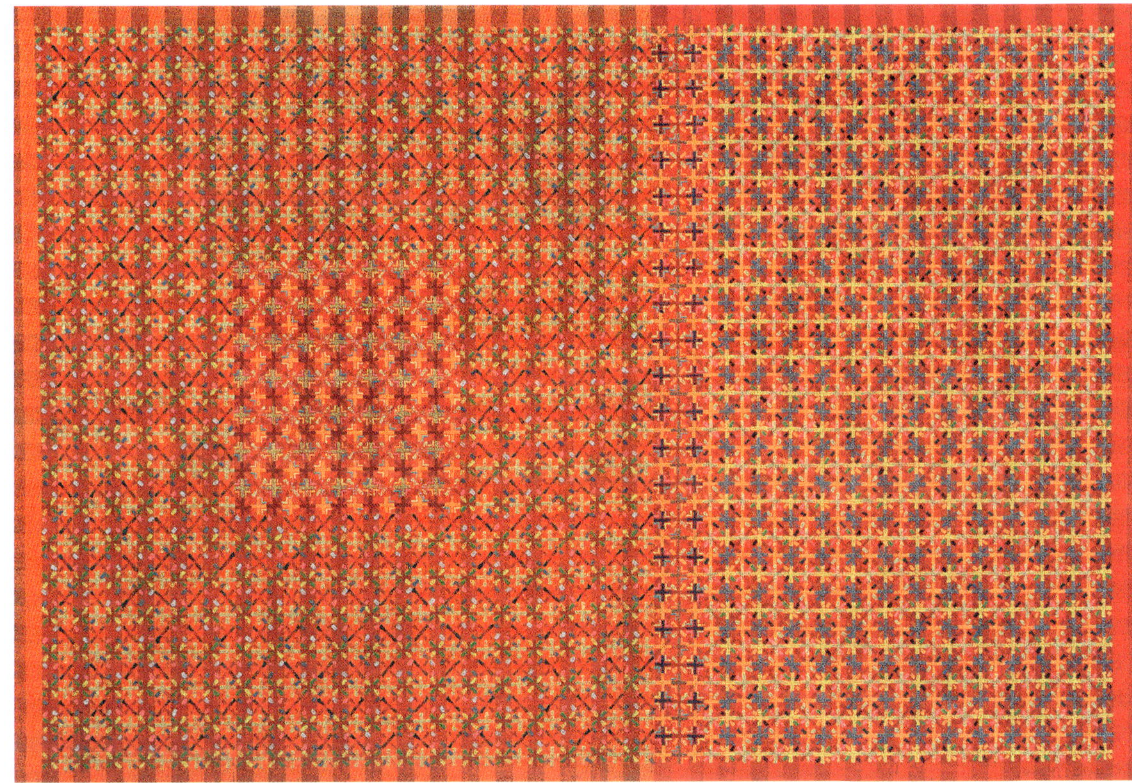

Appearance of Crosses 2000-9
(Scale 1:10)

十示 2000-9
(比例尺 1:10)

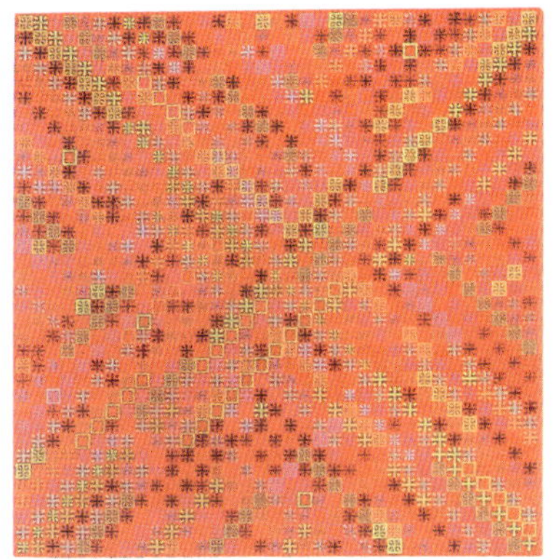

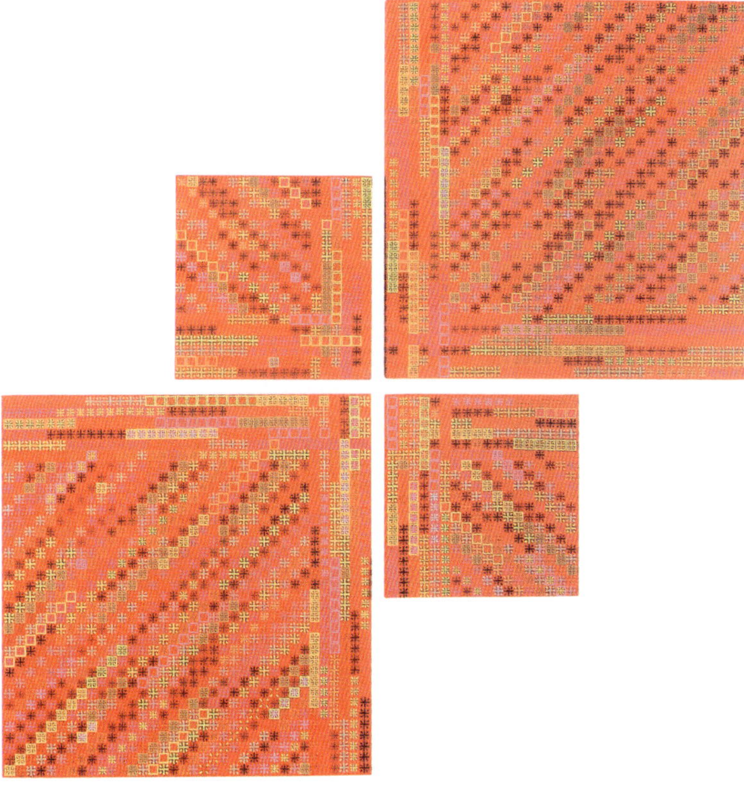

Appearance of Crosses 2008-21
(Scale 1:25)

十示 2008-21
(比例尺 1:25)

the first Treaty Ports some twenty years later, plaid cloth had been recast as a distinctive export product.

These historical associations on some level fed into Ding's later use of tartan textiles: 'The representation of social and culturally critical elements grew […] I wanted to touch issues such as "intercultural misreading" in my works.'[13] The reds, yellows and greens used by Ding echo those of existing tartan designs, and the arrangement of the grids suggests conventions of textile patternmaking – borders, grounds and motifs – that have somehow come adrift from their dominant symmetry. These works suggest products of a new hybridity, in which the global marketplace has become a cultural echo chamber of appropriations and misreadings.

By 2002, still sometimes working on tartan, Ding's works moved yet further beyond the realms of static, fixed patterns, increasingly acquiring a suggestion of motion: 'I wanted to demonstrate the clamour and excitement of this city in my works with fluorescent colours reflecting the materialised prosperity and fashionableness and the chaos and nihility behind the crosses'.[14] In some paintings, vertical bands scud downwards like scrolling electronic billboards, or tumbling shapes in an electronic game. In others there is a sense of the rush hour, with the centre of the canvas becoming a junction point with strips of coloured crosses streaking towards and away from it. The junction sequence reaches its ultimate expression in multi-panel works such as *Appearance of Crosses 2008-21* (see p. 39). The shock of the white cross of wall that emerges between this grouping of panels finds an echo in the gouged intersections of Ding's most recent series: in both there is a sense of exposure that comes almost like an explosive spark amid the suggestion of dynamic motion.

The works on show here in London, *Appearance of Crosses 2016-4 – 2016-10*, continue his unwavering exploration of abstraction and pattern-generation in relation to notions of the city, to design histories and to craft traditions, while perhaps also reflecting his knowledge and experience of working on textiles. From afar, they suggest magnified cloth – perhaps tweed or tartan – with the cross-markings standing in for the interlacing of warp and weft, and the scattered patches of colour hinting at a wider pattern. Under intimate scrutiny the complex layers of marks in different colours and lustres, and the new depth created by carving, suggest a tightly woven textile-like field. By learning about and employing woodblock carving he revisits and expands his interest in traditional craft forms and techniques, which include 'wood carving, bas relief, seal cutting, inscription, and carved polychrome lacquer'. Rather than making a woodblock work per se, however, Ding uses these skills in the service of his painting practice in order to generate 'a more dynamic role […] For me, to experiment with different materials is a method to explore painting, as well as to break through my own painting language.'[15]

第一个通商口岸，格纹布料成为了特色出口产品。

在某种层面上，这些历史联系渗入了丁乙后期对于格子布的使用："在这个阶段作品里开始有更多、更直接的社会和文化批判成分的体现。[…] 我想尝试在创作的方法上去触及如'文化间的误读'等问题。"[13]丁乙使用的红色、黄色和绿色呼应了成品格子布的设计。网格的安排则暗指纺织品制版的传统（包括围边、表面和花纹）出现了变化，不再完全对称。这些作品像是新的混合产物，而全球市场则变成了挪用和误读的文化回音室。

2002年，丁乙仍然会不时的使用格子布。但他的作品进一步超越了静止、固定的样式，日益明显的展示出运动感。"我想在作品里反映出这个城市的喧哗和刺激。荧光色和金属色折射了物质化的时尚和繁荣，但十字背后也可以看到混沌与虚无"。[14]有些作品中，粗线条竖直的从上往下掠过画布，像是转动的电子广告牌，或是电子游戏里翻滚的方块。另外一些作品中，观者会有交通高峰期的感觉，画布的中心是一个交叉点，有些彩色十字组成的长条向着中心点延伸，有些长条从中心向外发散。这样的交叉排列在《十示 2008-21》（见第39页）等多幅组合的作品中达到了极致。组画挂在墙上时，其排列方式使露出的墙体呈现白色十字状。这种让人震撼的体验类似他最新作品中把画板划开而成的交叉：两者都带有一种暴露感，仿佛作品在充满活力的动态中迸发的火星。

本次伦敦展览展出的作品（《十示 2016-4》到《十示 2016-10》）归因于他对于抽象和模式生成与城市、设计史和手工艺传统这些概念之间关系的不断探索。它们或许也反映出他使用织物创作积累的知识和经验。从远处看，作品仿佛放大的布料（可能是粗花呢或格子布），十字标志替代了经线和纬线的交织。一个个分散的色块暗示出一个更加广阔的样式。如果观者仔细研究，作品中不同颜色和光泽的标记层层交织，纷繁复杂；刻划则带来了新的深度，就像一个细密的、织物一般的场域。通过了解和使用木版雕刻技法，他再次展现并提升了对"木雕、浅浮雕、篆刻、碑刻、漆器的剔犀"等传统工艺形式和技巧的兴趣。丁乙创作的并不是木刻作品，而是使用木刻的技法为绘画服务，以便"有更大的自由性和机动性。[…] 材料的变化一直是我对于绘画表象探索相适应的一种手段，所以在不同的时间都会选用不同材料来突破自身绘画的语言。"[15]

1 Interview with the author conducted via email, 23 March 2017
2 From 'A Conversation between Shane McCausland and Ding Yi', April 2015, in *Ding Yi: What's Left to Appear*, catalogue published on the occasion of the exhibition at the Long Museum, Shanghai (2015)
3 Marc Augé, *Non-Places: An Introduction to Supermodernity*, second edition (Verso Books, 2008)
4 Interview with the author via email, 23 March 2017
5 From 'A Conversation between Shane McCausland and Ding Yi'
6 Yi-Fu Tuan, *Space and Place: the Perspective of Experience* (University of Minnesota Press, 1977)
7 'A Ding Yi interview by Mathieu Borysevicz', *Art Changsha Ding Yi* (Hunan Fine Art Publishing House, 2013)
8 Cao Weijun, 'Ding Yi: The Magician of Crosses', *Yishu: Journal of Contemporary Chinese Art*, Vol 7, No. 5 (Sep–Oct 2008)
9 ibid.
10 ibid.
11 Interview with the author via email, 23 March 2017
12 Robert Ross, *Clothing: A Global History* (Polity Press, Cambridge, 2008)
13 Cao Weijun, preparatory interview with Ding Yi, 10 November 2007 (unpublished)
14 ibid.
15 Interview with the author via email, 23 March 2017

1 和本文作者的电邮采访，2017年3月23日
2 引自《马啸鸿对话丁乙》，2015年4月，见《丁乙：何所示》，上海龙美术馆展览画册（2015年）
3 马克 · 奥吉（Marc Augé），《非场所：超现代性导论》，第二版 (Verso Books, 2008年）
4 和本文作者的电邮采访，2017年3月23日
5 引自《马啸鸿对话丁乙》
6 段义孚，《空间与场所：经验的视角》，（明尼苏达大学出版社，1977年）
7 《丁乙采访（马修·伯利塞维兹 Mathieu Borysevicz）》，载于《2013艺术长沙：丁乙》（湖南美术出版社，2013年）
8 曹维君，《"十"的魔术师》，载于《典藏国际版》（*Yishu: Journal of Contemporary Chinese Art*），Vol 7, No. 5（2008年9月-10月）
9 同上
10 同上
11 和本文作者的电邮采访，2017年3月23日
12 罗伯特 · 罗斯（Robert Ross），《服装：全球史》(Polity Press，剑桥，2008年）
13 曹维君，《跟丁乙闲聊》，2007年11月10日（未出版）
14 同上
15 和本文作者的电邮采访，2017年3月23日

Crosstalk: A Brief History of Ding Yi

Martin Herbert

In 1986, a year when he was majoring in Chinese ink painting at Shanghai University and occasionally engaging in performance art, Ding Yi made a painting entitled *Taboo* – in retrospect, it looks like a premonition. The painting, executed in fluently unbuttoned brushwork, features a central rectangle divided by an X, the subsections themselves teeming with smaller X's. The twenty-four-year-old Ding's style here appears indebted to German Neo-Expressionism, its mix of stern greys and warm metallic tones particularly recalling the work of Albert Oehlen and Martin Kippenberger, and Ding has said in interviews that one primary influence on the vaunted '85 New Wave movement in Chinese art was, indeed, Expressionism and its descendants. The other stimulus, he reckons, was Surrealism, which 'offers a broad path in that it can be extremely abstract and filled with imagination.'[1] In the ensuing years, as Ding developed a body of painting that displays the diverse associative properties of that one symbol – the cross – Expressionism would fall away; using that symbol over and over might even be considered the *opposite* of expressiveness. Abstraction filled with imagination, however, would become his mainstay.

We might trace the X back further in Ding's life, to the fact that as a young man he worked in a printing factory. In printing the X is used to measure up a surface, dividing an area into many squares through a distribution of crosses upon it. That is, we *might* make

十示谈:丁乙略传

马丁·赫伯特

1986年,丁乙在上海大学读国画,偶尔创作行为艺术。那年,他画了一幅油画,名叫《禁忌》。如今看来,这仿佛一个预兆。作品笔触随性。画面正中的方块上画了一个大"X",由此形成的几个区间中遍布小"X"。当时丁乙二十四岁。这件作品的风格似乎借鉴了德国新表现主义,混合了银灰色和暖金属色调,让人想起阿尔伯特·厄伦(Albert Oehlen)和马丁·基彭伯格(Martin Kippenberger)的作品。丁乙在受访时曾说过,表现主义和其衍生的各类主义正是中国艺术"八五新潮"的两个主要影响因素之一。他认为,另一个诱因是超现实主义,因为它"线路的宽度很宽;它是可以非常抽象的,非常充满想象的方式"[1]。之后几年里,丁乙创作了一系列油画,展示出"十字"符号能带来多元联想,与表现主义渐行渐远。重复使用这一符号甚至可以说是对表现性的背离。充满想象的抽象成为他创作的支柱。

"X"符号或许可以追溯到丁乙更早的人生经历。他年轻时在印刷厂工作过。印刷中,"X"用于测量,数个十字分布在纸面上,把纸面分成数个方块。我们可能把这段人生经历看成影响他的因素;我们也可以说,在印刷过程中,"X"和印

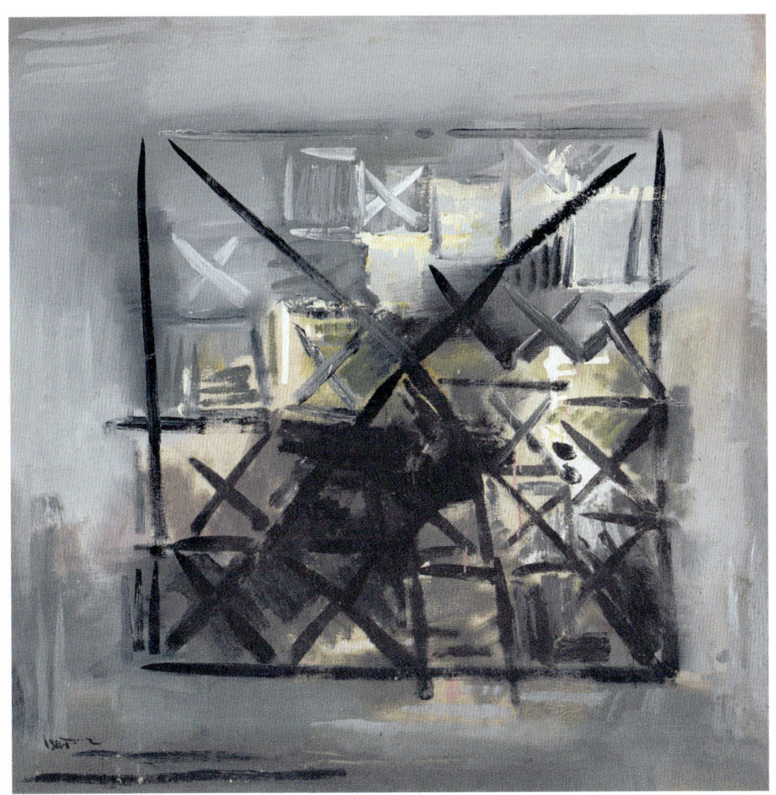

Taboo
(Scale 1:7)

禁忌
(比例尺 1:7)

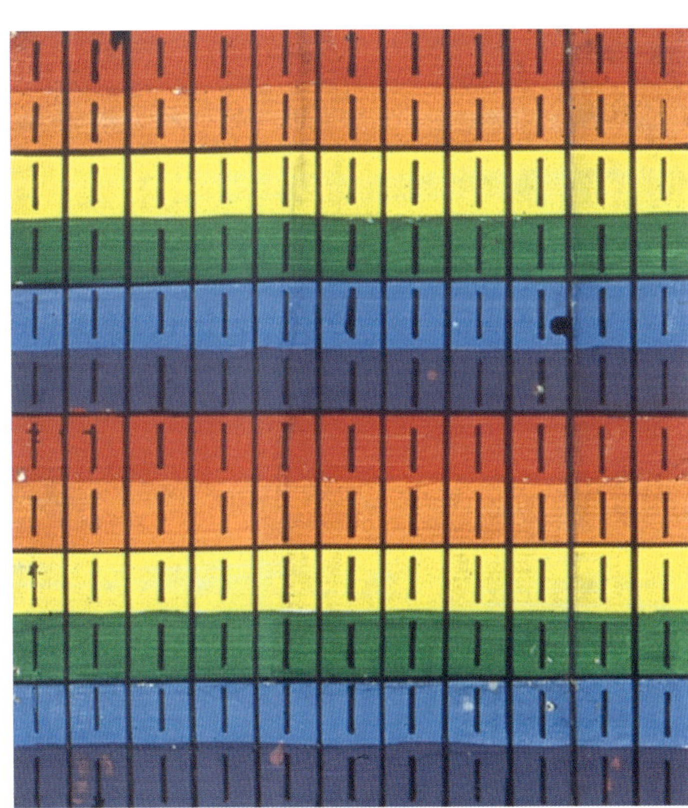

Draft 1987
(Scale 1:2)

手稿 1987
(比例尺 1:2)

this formative autobiographical connection; or we might consider that the X, in the making of a print, stands in relation to whatever is printed as an open signifier, and indeed for Ding the appeal of the X is that outwardly it *doesn't* mean anything. (He also decided to stick with it, so he's said, out of a need to pursue simplicity, after simultaneously studying Western Modernism and traditional Chinese painting techniques, and wanting – if possible – to eliminate direct aesthetic influence from either side.) In his work, the cross can come to suggest many things at once, while being tied to none of them. X, like the factor it names, is multiform, slippery, near paradoxical: it doesn't mean anything, yet somehow comes to encompass everything.

The year after painting *Taboo*, and while divesting himself of those vestiges of expressivity, Ding began the *Appearance of Crosses* series that would become his life's work. Tentatively at first: *Draft 1987* (see p. 43), on paper, is a grid of rainbow-coloured cells – pointedly non-expressive in choice of colours – each containing a vertical slit. The grid is nascent, the painting abstract if somewhat urbanite, the brushwork tightened significantly. Two years later, Ding had found himself. *Appearance of Crosses 1989-7* is an intricate interlacing of upright and diagonal grids: white dashes percolate around a red lattice like perfectly spaced traffic, while each section of the matrix is filled with a nested pattern of darker diagonals, their centres glowing orange.

刷内容之间构成了一个开放的能指关系。实际上，吸引丁乙的正是“X”表面上没有任何意义。（他说过，他同时学习了西方现代主义和国画技巧，希望尽可能消除两者直接的美学影响，力求简洁，因此决定沿用这一符号。）在他的作品中，十字可以同时代表很多东西，却不会有任何明确关联。“X”和它所代表的未知因素形式多样，模棱两可，几近自相矛盾：这个符号毫无意义，却包罗万象。

《禁忌》画完后一年，丁乙继续抹去作品中表现性的痕迹，开始创作《十示》系列，由此开启了他的毕生之作。最初的作品有试探性质：《手稿 1987》（见第43页）中，多种颜色的单元构成了一个网格（作品用色明确的背离了表现性），单元正中各有一条竖线。作品中，网格初具形态。作品风格抽象，又有些许新潮，笔触明显紧凑了许多。两年后，他找到了感觉。《十示 1989-7》构图精细，水平和竖直的网格交错：红色方格四边嵌有白色短线，像摆放整齐的车辆；矩阵中的每个网格内都有数个大小嵌套的竖直方块，颜色更深，中心亮橙色。显然，西方作品中最相近的类比是《百老汇爵士乐》

The closest Western analogue here is, surely, *Broadway Boogie-Woogie* (1942–3), Piet Mondrian's nonfigurative translation of the excitement of New York, and the Dutch modernist was indeed an influence on Ding (who didn't, in fact, completely manage to avoid being imprinted by existing art); equally so, as Manhattan was for Mondrian, was the vivacity and confusion of Shanghai itself. And yet this painting is not exactly of Shanghai (which nevertheless becomes a more overt point of reference later in Ding's work). To a viewer, it might just feel temporarily like a refracting of the city and then revert to what it is, a highly controlled abstraction that would be unearthly if it weren't – thanks to all manner of small variances in the brushwork, and despite Ding's use of certain mechanical tools to downplay his selfhood – still visibly handmade.

Over the next few years, as if showing off a jewel's facets, Ding would demonstrate the multiform associative potential of this structurally equivocal approach, putting enough clashing associations into his work that, contrarily, it *had* to read as abstraction because it couldn't be all the things it recalled. While switching his colour emphasis to green in 1990's *Appearance of Crosses 1990-5*, he seems for a moment to suspend us over an evenly tree-studded park – until the painting goes back to being a grid structured on cross-based glyphs, albeit ones that almost look like refugees from an arcade game.

（Broadway Boogie-Woogie，1942-1943年），荷兰现代主义艺术家皮特·蒙德里安（Piet Mondrian）对热闹纽约的非具象诠释。蒙德里安的确影响了丁乙的创作（实际上，丁乙也无法完全摆脱艺术史的印记）。同样，曼哈顿和蒙德里安的关系相当于活跃纷繁的上海之于丁乙。但这件作品画的并不全是上海（上海在丁乙后期作品中将成为更明确的参照点）。观者可能在瞬间感觉看到了作品折射出的城市，然后就会回归到它的本原：一件高度严谨的抽象作品。因为可以清晰察觉手工的痕迹，作品才不会有不食人间烟火的感觉。（虽然他使用了某种工具以降低作品的自我特性，但笔法中能看出各种细微的差异。）

之后几年，丁乙展示出这种模糊结构的创作方式具有多种形式的组合可能，仿佛一件珠宝的各个刻面。他在作品中放入大量相互矛盾的组合。结果是，作品不可能代表其所有能联想到的事物，必须要抽象解读。1990年的《十示 1990-5》的主色变成了绿色，初看好似鸟瞰种着整齐树木的公园，之后画面再度呈现为基于十字符号的网格结构，这些符号几乎就像街机游戏里的流民。整件作品也可以说像一块地毯。一年之后

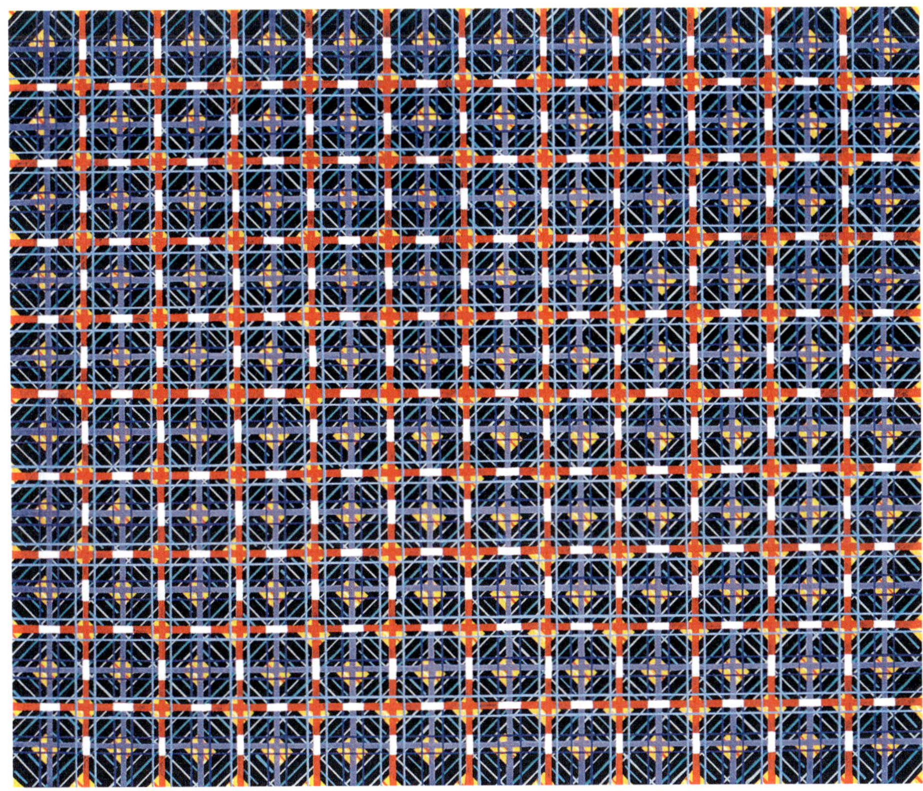

Appearance of Crosses 1989 - 7
(Scale 1:10)

十示 1989 - 7
(比例尺 1:10)

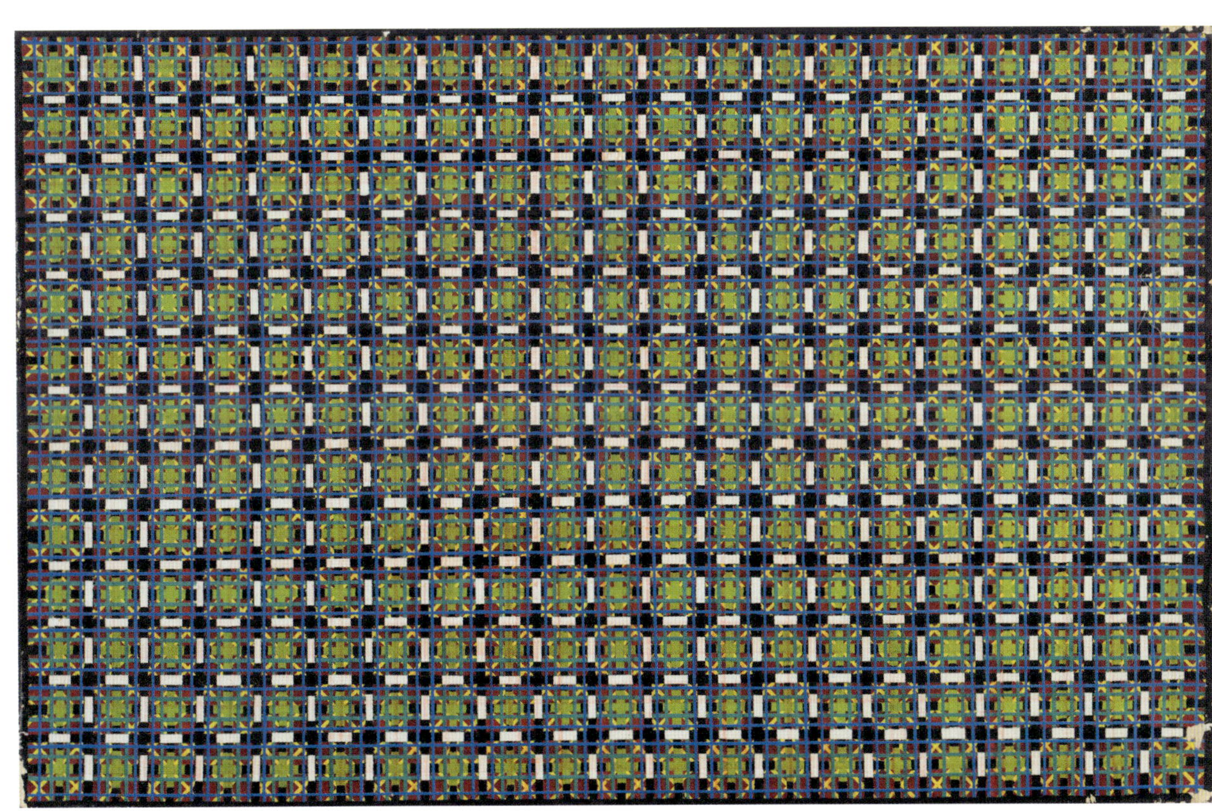

Appearance of Crosses 1990 - 5
(Scale 1:10)

十示 1990 - 5
(比例尺 1:10)

Alternatively, the whole thing might resemble some kind of rug. The textile codification would be more emphatic in the following year's *Appearance of Crosses 1991-3*, with its scintillating, Op-like interlace of hot colours woven amid a fine white grid. Containing all manner of complexly decentred patterning – some of which a viewer might 'see', some of which might merely be imagined – it looks like hyper-advanced tartan. And indeed, by 1997 Ding would be painting *on* tartan itself, and by 2008 he'd be collaborating with luxury scarf-makers Hermès.

But it's worth rewinding a bit here and then continuing chronologically to show just how fast Ding was travelling, how much he could pull into his seemingly tightly circumscribed orbit. The 1991 painting just mentioned has, I would say, no implicit scale: it just *is*, unless the scale is that of a piece of pre-existing material and this is a 1:1 copy of it. Another work from the same year, *Appearance of Crosses 1991-7*, looks like candy-coloured TV static and a rag rug at once, the brush marks – as ever, a mix of X's and +'s – appearing woven. The vibe of balanced attention seems to be a product of Ding's working method, which he's compared to playing the game of Go – 'from spot to line and line develops into pattern… take the centre, take the corner!'[2] And while the work has a tonality, a bright, purplish-green, artificial mood, it also appears that you could locate any colour within its mesh, linking the work back to the earliest parts of Ding's series, where he appeared intent on personality removal via a non-discriminating spectrum of colours as well as non-expressive application.

It's hard not to talk about what one sees – particularly as someone who doesn't live in urban China and has only visited briefly – in these paintings, and hard to persuade someone else of your opinions' importance. The perpetual interplay of various interpretations, though, might count for something. *Appearance of Crosses 1992-15* (see p. 49) suggests countless angelfish swimming in tight formation within a darkened aquarium, also stained glass, also a kaleidoscope – but that's just me, and the colours, putting together completely unrelated worldly things. It's a coloured grid, an abstraction. The things I see aren't valuable – what *might* be, philosophically, is the painting's ability to be many things at once, to suggest that differences between things count for less than similarities. (Ding mostly doesn't push an explicit worldview forward in his work, but one might hazard that the concept of interconnectedness that runs through various Chinese metaphysical traditions is in there somewhere.) And what might really be important, on various levels, is that it all starts from one thing. Ed Ruscha titled a 1977 painting *No End to the Things Made Out of Human Talk.* Ding Yi might say the same, but it's not human talk – it's that cruciform he began with, that little thing that's become so big.

的《十示 1991-3》看起来更像一块织物，在工整的白色网格中交织着各种亮色，欧普（Op）般的交错风格妙趣横生。它包括了各种偏移画面中心的图示（观者可能会“看见”一些图示，有些图示可能要靠想象），像一块十分亮丽的苏格兰格子布。实际上，1997年，丁乙会把作品画在格子布上。2008年，他则会和生产丝巾的奢侈品牌爱马仕合作。

回到九十年代：丁乙在飞速的前进，进入自己构建的看似限制严格的轨道。我认为，上文提及的1991年作品尺寸毫不含蓄，大的怡然自得；仿佛有一块现成的布料，而这件作品是布料1:1的复制品。同一年的另外一件作品《十示 1991-7》像糖果色的电视杂讯，也像碎布地毯。作品笔触（仍然是“X”和“+”的混合）好似编织而成。作品整体效果均衡，是丁乙创作方式的产物。他把这种方式比作下围棋：“从点到线，线到面……先画中心，再画四边”[2]。这件作品的色调统一，有亮紫青色的人造氛围，但观者好像可以在网格里找到各种颜色，联想到丁乙早期的系列作品。早期作品中，他希望抹去个性，平均选择各种颜色，以非表现性的方式上色。

观者会情不自禁的谈论在丁乙作品中看到些什么（尤其像我这样的人，不住在中国城市里，只是偶尔去中国），也很难说服别人，让他们觉得你的观点很重要。不过，连绵不断的多种阐释交织可能会有其价值。《十示 1992-15》（见第49页）看似无穷无尽的神仙鱼在昏暗的水族馆中成群游动，紧密相依。它也像彩色玻璃，或万花筒——但这只是我的感觉，在看到这些颜色之后联想到各种完全无关的事物。它是一个上色的网格，一种抽象。我看到什么不重要。哲学上可能重要的是，作品能同时呈现多种面貌，暗示出事物的相同之处大于差异。（大体上，丁乙不想通过作品体现某种明确的世界观。但我们可以大胆假设，作品的某些地方仍可以看出中国各类形而上传统中一以贯之的关联性。）在各个层面上，真正重要的大概在于，他的创作全部源于一个符号。埃德·拉斯查（Ed Ruscha）把一幅1977年的油画命名为《人类对话无穷的解读》（No End to the Things Made Out of Human Talk）。丁乙也可以如是说，但这里解读的不再是人类对话，而是他一开始就在用的十字。小十字发展出了大意义。

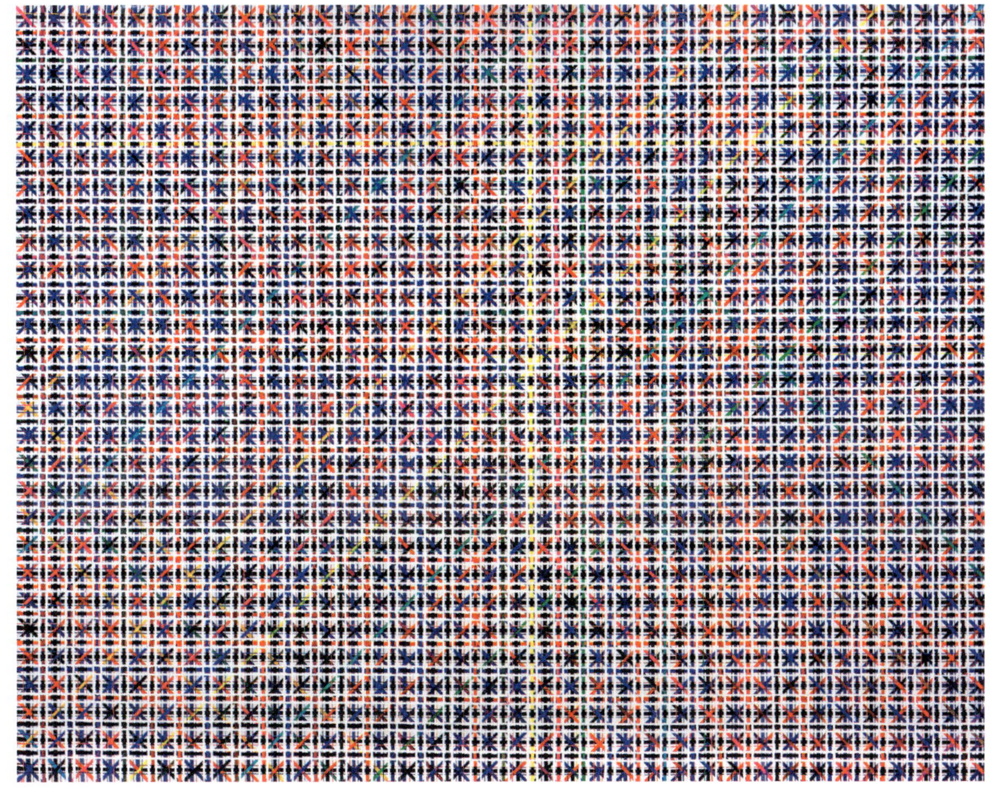

Appearance of Crosses 1991 - 3
(Scale 1:15)

十示 1991 - 3
(比例尺 1:15)

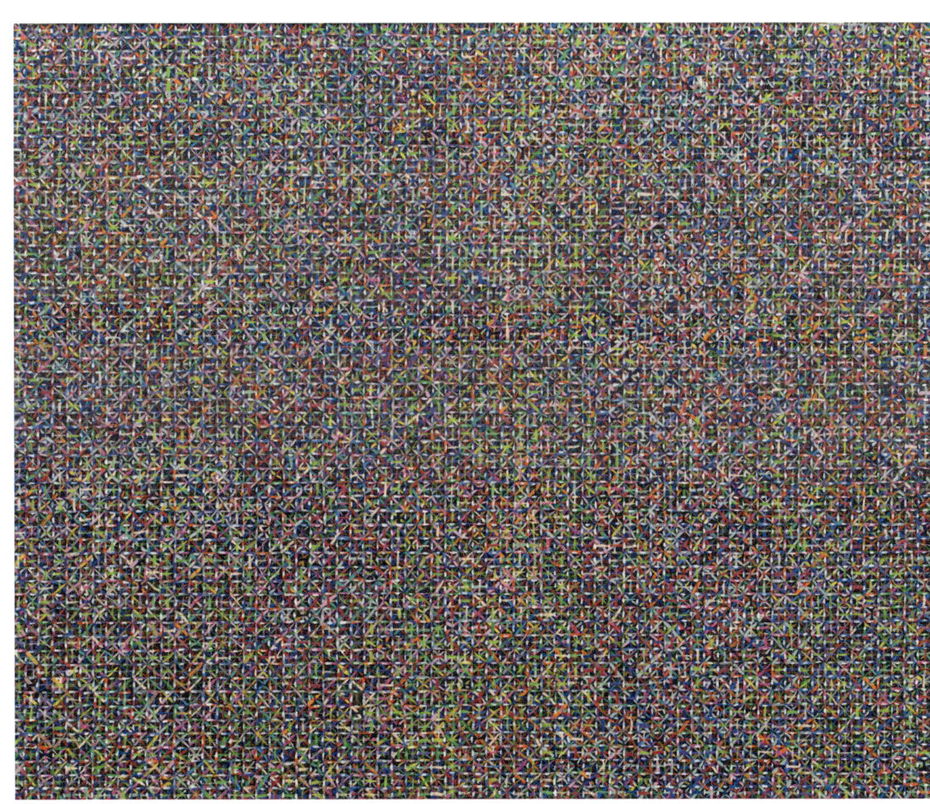

Appearance of Crosses 1991 - 7
(Scale 1:15)

十示 1991 - 7
(比例尺 1:15)

If Mondrian did indeed have bearing on these works, another point of comparison – though not one Ding has brought up – might be the early work of Agnes Martin, not least for her ability to run virtuoso variations on the narrow theme of the grid. (See, from Ding, 1992's *Appearance of Crosses 1992-20,* which switches into monochrome, black and white and greys with no drop in energy, and conveys a sci-fi feel.) The American painter's work might also be recalled by Ding's decision, around here, to pull back the edges of his grids so that they sit on the canvas, this being the reverse in fact of what Martin did herself: in the 1960s she went from 'on' to 'all-over'. *Appearance of Crosses 1995-29* (see p. 51) exemplifies this new if temporary mode in Ding's art, being a hot, orangey-red, wavering grid rendered in charcoal and chalk, an abstract sunset – or, again, condensation of metropolitan energy – whose edges peter out before the edge of the linen it's painted on, conveying the illusion of a piece of woven fabric *on* a canvas surface. Instability, here, was being enacted on the level of the artwork itself. The word 'appearance' in the English translation of Ding's standard title, we might note at this point, has itself a double meaning: manifestation, and also façade.

By 1997 the issues of ontology playing out in Ding's art had been twisted anew. (Indeed, one thing that should be clear is that he is *forever* twisting his art anew: outside of his fixed icons, change is his main consistency – and this, we'll see, also has worldly resonances.) Where he'd previously simulated tartan – or verged on doing so – now he was painting *on* tartan, a readymade colour grid that teases historical associations without resolving them, and raising the question of where his work began and the tartan-maker's ended. Ding fills the Burberry tan squares of the plaid in *Appearance of Crosses 1997-4* (see p. 51) in toothpaste shades, aquamarine and pink, and overlays them with a grid of tadpole-like blobs – an incommensurable field of associations once again, to the point that they begin cancelling each other out.

Ding's art was becoming, by this point, a self-reflexive system. Not only was he demonstrating how various one could be with a tightly attenuated iconographic range, he was also apparently reversing on – reacting to – himself. Up until now his paintings had taken one form and multiplied it; they'd been approximately symmetrical and distributed. By 2001's *Appearance of Crosses 2001-1* (see p. 53) (still on tartan and predominantly green-hued if far from natural-looking) this was a rule ripe to be broken. The painting divides into two distinct halves, patterning playing out differently on each – the right's distinct squares a little like regimented grave markers; the left, whose knotted crosses have a rotational feel, hosting another inset square with a shimmering grid of its own.

假如可以说蒙德里安影响了丁乙的创作，美国画家艾格尼丝·马丁（Agnes Martin）的早期作品也可以和丁乙的作品比较（虽然他并未谈论过马丁）。最明显的一点是：她专注网格这一有限的主题，却可以玩出多种花样。（参照丁乙1992年的作品《十示 1992-20》。作品转而使用黑白灰等单色，仍然充满能量和科幻感。）另外一个可比的是：丁乙在那段时间决定把网格的四边拉回到画布之上。这和马丁的做法正好相反：1960年代，她的边界从画布“之上”变成了画布“四周”。《十示 1995-29》（见第51页）是这个短暂的新发展的例证：粉笔和炭笔画出摇曳的橙红色网格，像抽象的日落，抑或是都市能量的浓缩。笔触在抵达亚麻布的四边时渐次减少，仿佛盖在画布表面上的一块布。作品本身带来了不稳定性。“十示”中的“示”对应的英文翻译是“appearance”，这里可以有双重理解：显现和表象。

1997年，丁乙作品中呈现的本体论问题有了新的转变。（实际上，我想说明一点：他一直在创作中引入新的变化。除了恒定的符号，他一直在变。我们会发现，这一点也有其尘世的回响。）之前，有些作品看起来像格子布。这一年，他开始在格子布上创作。格子布是现成的彩色网格，戏谑地暗指其历史关联，却不会消解这些关联。这让人想问：他的作品从何处开始？格子布生产商的工作在何处终结？《十示 1997-4》（见第51页）画在博柏利（Burberry）苏格兰格子布上。丁乙在棕褐色的方块里填入各类牙膏色、蓝绿和粉红色，在方格上叠加了蝌蚪状斑点组成的网格——由此带来大量不同的联想，数量多到开始互相抵消。

此时，丁乙的艺术已经成为一套自我指涉的体系。他展示出，使用极少的图形符号可以呈现出多样的结果。他也开始回应自我，尝试新方法。之前，他的作品基于同一图示，大量重复；它们近乎对称、分布均匀。到了2001年，作品《十示 2001-1》（见第53页）打破了这个规则（仍然画在了格子布上，主色调是除自然的草绿之外的各种绿色）。画面清晰地分成了两半，各有不同的图形构造。右半边的方块有些像排列整齐的墓地纪念碑；左半边结状的十字好像在转动，正中插入一个颜色闪亮的正方形网格。他已经画了十五年十字。每一幅作品都说明，他不再需要任何其它元素。

Appearance of Crosses 1992 - 15
(Scale 1:15)

十示 1992 - 15
(比例尺 1:15)

Appearance of Crosses 1992 - 20
(Scale 1:20)

十示 1992 - 20
(比例尺 1:20)

He'd been painting crosses for fifteen years now. Each painting said that he needed nothing else.

Those who believe that our world is, in fact, a simulation set in play by higher beings – not so far, of course, from a belief in God – sometimes point to the fact that all matter is at base geometric. Everything is made up of regularly shaped building blocks, and patterns recur – fractals, for instance – on different scales. One can make a more directly theistic response to this and say that nature is an endless recombination of basic elements – we're composed of them and one day we'll go back into the ground, return to the great circulatory system, and make more things, just as we're made from former things – atoms dating back to stardust. Something of this reverberates through Ding's paintings, with their insistence on simple building blocks to create a boggling multiplicity of results. Look at *Appearance of Crosses 2002-2* (see p. 53), another green-hued painting. (At some point, Ding's palette gravitated towards red and green, the colours of the stock market. Naturally he said this was a coincidence.) Ask, first, *where* we are. Yes, we're in a painting. But we could be looking down on a forest, we could have our noses pressed up against blades of grass, we could be looking at something digital, or something stitched, or something – of course – hand-painted. We could be looking at data. Truth be told, we're really looking at crosses and mostly projecting the rest.

有人认为，我们的世界实际上是更高等生物模拟出的宇宙（这其实和信上帝差别不大）。他们时常会说，所有物质本质都是几何。万事万物由形状规整的构件组成。同样的模式会重复出现在不同的尺度上（分形就是一个例子）。我们也可以对这个观点做出更直接的、有神论的回应，即自然是基本元素的无穷尽的再组合。我们由这些基本元素组成。终有一天，我们会尘归尘、土归土，回归那宏大的循环系统，让系统继续创造万事万物。构成我们的元素也是由过去的事物分解而成——原子可以追溯到星尘。丁乙作品中回荡着这些观念的片段。他坚持用简单元素构建出让人难以想象的多样结果。以《十示 2002-2》（见第53页）为例，这幅油画的主色调也是绿色。（有一段时间，丁乙的用色偏向股市的标志色：红和绿。当然，他说这只是偶然。）首先要问的是，我们在哪里？我们在一幅画中。但是，我们看到的也可以是一座森林的鸟瞰图、贴近看的草叶、数码图案、一块编织物，或是（自然而然地想到的）手绘作品。我们看到的也可能是数据。但实际上，我们真正看到的是大量十字。其它内容都是我们内心的投射。

That said, perhaps one should consider 'absence of definite content' as another nostrum Ding might be subverting. Abstraction, Mondrian would be the first to remind us, partakes of the world – he began with trees, after all – and one might consider Ding's own rapid, self-renovating development of his painting as a kind of analogue for his home continent's own transformation over the same period: a kind of meta-commentary, painting – once again – as model, this time on the abstraction-of-sorts that was China's modernisation. One writer, meanwhile, describes the experience of a Ding painting – made in the world's most populous city – as of being 'shouted at by a crowd of people'.[3]

There were more definite signs of rootedness, too. By 1998, he had begun to introduce neon colours into his work. This, he's said, was a direct response to the urban texture of Shanghai, to the city's rapid development in the '90s as a result of Deng Xiaoping's economic reforms, and its gaudy festooning with artificial lights, a literal beacon of China's growth. To an extent, though, Ding had been thrust in this direction from outside. In '98 a Canadian art historian had visited his studio and asked how his paintings could *not* be responsive to place at a time when the city he worked in was undergoing such extreme transformation, and Ding took this on board: 'I felt before that my painting didn't relate so much with the Chinese society I lived in.'[4] Built into his use of a neon palette, he's clarified,

虽然如此，我们大概也可以说，"明确内容缺失"可能也是丁乙要推翻的一个"秘诀"。抽象是入世的：蒙德里安应该是这个理念的最大支持者（他最早作品的主题是树木）。我们可以认为，丁乙的创作在迅速的自我革新，类似于他的祖国同期的转变：一种衍生评论，（再一次）以中国现代化的某种抽象为模型的绘画。同时，一名评论家看到丁乙（在全球人口最多的城市里创作的）作品后，说感觉像"一群人在我周边叫嚷着"[3]。

丁乙的创作也有更明确体现"根基"的标记。到了1998年，他开始在作品中使用霓虹色。他说，这是对于上海城市肌理的直接反映，回应了九十年代邓小平经济改革后城市的迅速发展。艳俗花哨的灯箱装饰随处可见，好似中国增长的灯塔。虽然，在某种程度上，丁乙被外力推到了这个方向。1998年，一名加拿大艺术史学家访问他的画室。他问艺术家，上海正经历如此巨大的变革，他的作品怎么能不对他们生活的社会表示态度。丁乙后来采纳了这一意见。"我之前觉得，我的作品和我所生活的社会没有多大关联。"[4] 通过使用各种霓虹色，这些作品明确嵌入了些许批判：霓虹灯的光不是自然光。他对（以上海为典范的）中国

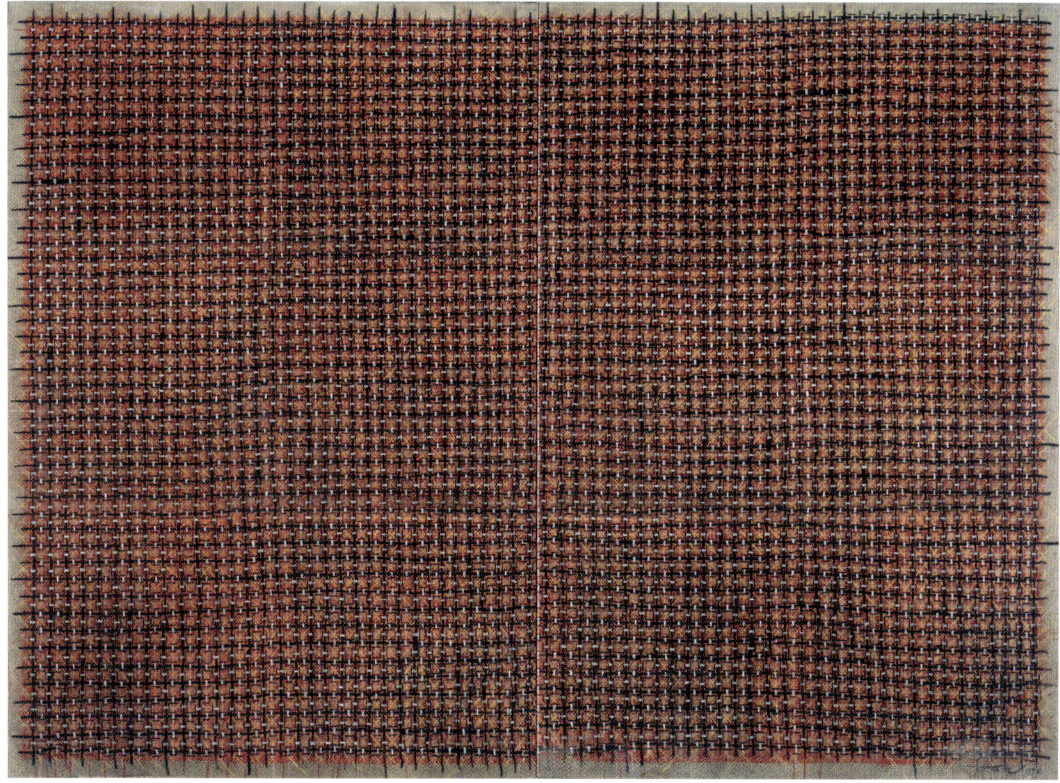

Appearance of Crosses 1995 - 29
(Scale 1:20)

十示 1995 - 29
(比例尺 1:20)

Appearance of Crosses 1997 - 4
(Scale 1:15)

十示 1997 - 4
(比例尺 1:15)

is a glimmering critique: neon light is not natural light, and the urbanisation of China's cities – of which Shanghai is exemplary – is, he's said, 'not something rooted firmly in the ground, nor something with a solid core; it is a superficial thing.'[5] That we might look at one of Ding's paintings and ask what is *really,* solidly there, then, is no longer just a formal issue, but one that begins to loop the work back – once again – to the painter's real-world experience: is this all a mirage?

The paintings he made over the next few years thus perpetuate ambiguous multiplicity with latent reason. Most of all they deliver the effect of almost claustrophobic proximity and vaulting distance at once. We feel right up against bright lights (Ding's colours are those of 'Shanghai at night', he's also said)[6] and pressed against some kind of opulent, warmly coloured fabric (made in China?) and also suspended hundreds of feet above a landscape. The quirks of reception depend what kinds of imagery you're familiar with, including technological ones. *Appearance of Crosses 2003 - 9* (see p. 55), another warm-toned number on tartan, features an asymmetric distribution of orange, yellow, red and pink regions made up of clustered coloured asterisks: it could be thermal imagery, on any scale. *Appearance of Crosses 2008 - 2* (see p. 55), with its popping, scintillating red and yellow rows angled on the diagonal, brings us back to jazzy cityscapes (also microscopic cellular images, also pure pattern making). If Ding's city is now perpetually boogie-woogie-ing, that may not be all to the good; and that's before we even get onto the new modes of vision. He's also said that Shanghai makes him feel 'spiritually lost'[7] and that working with his cross-patterning, by contrast, restores to him a sense of calm. There's an intimation in this, inevitably, that his art might do the same for a metropolitan viewer, harassed in similar if not equal ways.

Yet too much information – too much directive-ness on the artist's part – can kill a work of art. Saying that his art relates to Shanghai is already quite a lot for Ding, and I think he can say it because his art turns on a duplicity of appearances. It might be the writer's job to say that such art feels continually relevant now because *reality* – not just in Shanghai – turns on the duplicity of appearances, and that the unpredictability of Ding's images is our own experience of being in the contemporary, careening world, where the mask of civilisation seems to slip a little further each day. To whom is it due that in his works from about 2010 onwards – such as *Appearance of Crosses 2010 - 2* (see p. 56), with its big, glowing yellow central X – I start seeing the crosses as gun sights? In the same year, Ding's palette shifts: it cools rapidly, the base turning darker and the lines going diagrammatic: in *Appearance of Crosses 2010 - 16* (see p. 56) we're launched into fathoms-deep space criss-crossed by flickering lines in greens and indigos, like some kind of provisional

城市化的看法是:"它不是一种根深蒂固的东西,不是一个核心的东西。[5]它是一种表皮的东西。"我们可能看着丁乙的一幅作品,想问里面到底有些什么。这说明,它不再仅是关于形式的问题,而是开始把作品(再次)带回画家的真实世界体验:这是否都是海市蜃楼?

丁乙之后几年的作品继续结合了模糊的多重性和隐匿的理性。最重要的是,作品同时体现了幽闭恐惧般的接近度和巨大的距离感。我们感觉近距离盯着明亮的灯光(他自己也说过,用色来自"夜上海"[6]),像看着某种华丽的暖色织物(是不是中国制造?),也像从几百英尺的上空鸟瞰风景。对于作品的反应取决于你熟悉哪些科学影像或是其它图像。《十示 2003-9》(见第55页)也是画在格子布上的暖色作品。画面上橙色、黄色、红色和粉色的星号聚集而成的区域呈不对称分布:它像一幅任何比例尺的热成像图。《十示 2008-2》(见第55页)的画面上,闪烁、跳跃的红色和黄色构成了对角线,把我们带回爵士乐般的城市风景(也可以是显微细胞图,或是纯粹的图式)。丁乙所在的城市一直沉浸在歌舞升平之中。但是,这是一种喜忧参半的发展,我们甚至还没来得及建立新视觉模式。他曾说过,上海让他感到"精神上迷失"[7]。相对的,用十字创作能帮他恢复平静的心情。他的作品对于都市的观者肯定有同样效果,因为他们也受到了同样或类似的困扰。

但是,太多的信息(艺术家体现出太多的定向性)会破坏作品。说他的艺术和上海有关联对于丁乙来说已经颇为不易。我认为,他可以这么说的原因在于,他的艺术取决于"示"的双重性。我想说,他的艺术创作一直都没有和时代脱节,因为现实(不仅在上海)也取决于"示"的双重性。丁乙作品图像的不可预见性代表了急速向前的当代社会。我们身处其中,文明的面具每一天都撕掉一点。由于谁的影响,让我在他2010年之后的作品中(例如2010年的《十示 2010-2》(见第56页)正中画着巨大的闪亮的黄色"X")开始觉得十字符号像瞄准镜?同一年,丁乙的用色变了:颜色冷了很多,底色变的灰暗,线条呈现图示感。在《十示 2010-16》(见第56页)中,闪烁的绿色和靛蓝色线条把我们送入了幽深的空间,像是某种临时的机器架构,或是一张数码素描,亦或像跳跃超空间。当然,所有的解读都是主观

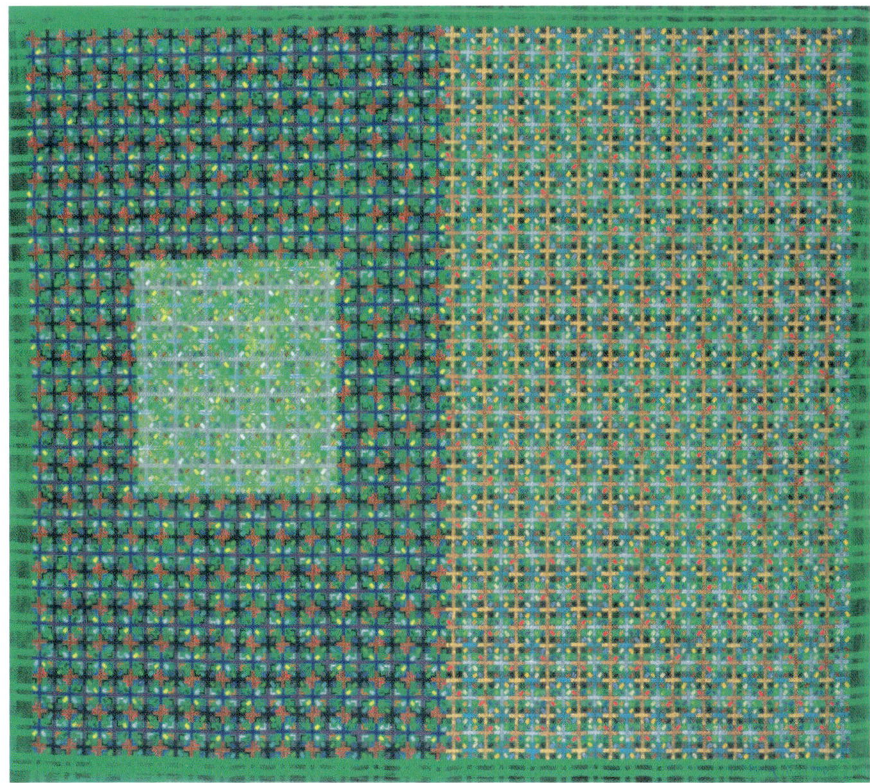

Appearance of Crosses 2001 - 1
(Scale 1:15)

十示 2001 - 1
(比例尺 1:15)

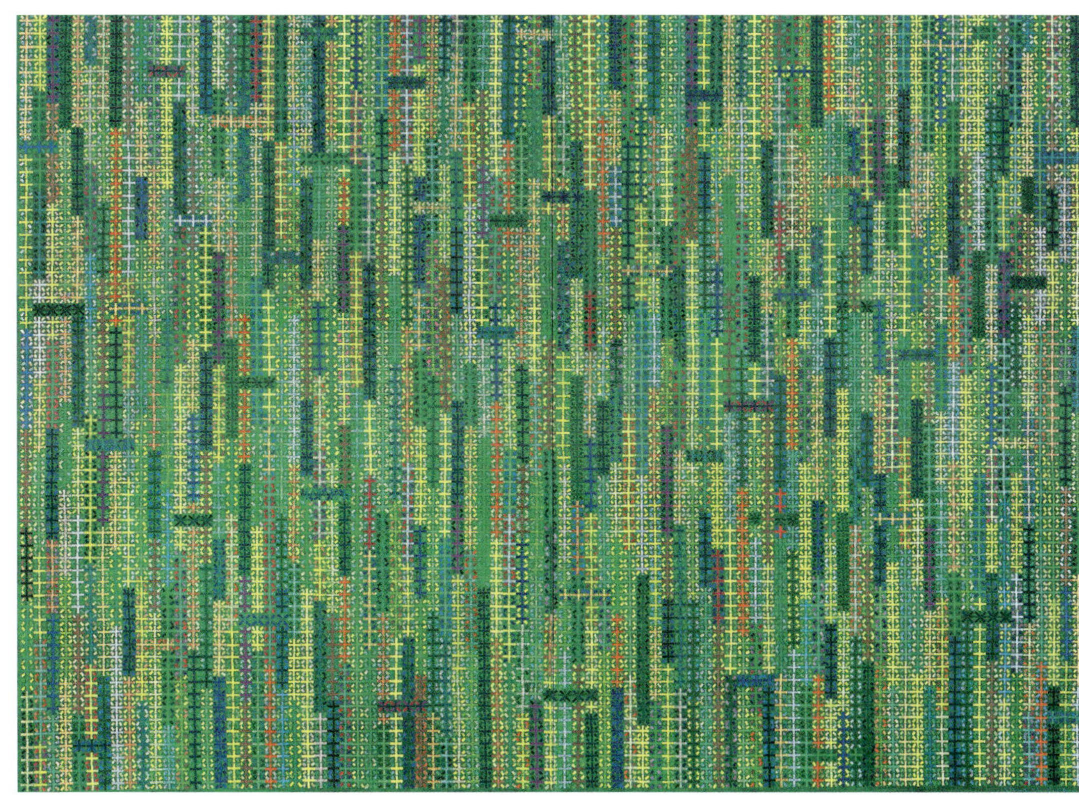

Appearance of Crosses 2002 - 2
(Scale 1:20)

十示 2002 - 2
(比例尺 1:20)

machine architecture, a digital sketch of something, or a leap through hyperspace. All interpretations are entirely subjective, of course: the point is that Ding's art lets them – almost makes them – exist.

Yet we seem to be shifting here from a human vision to some kind of technocratic vision: *Appearance of Crosses 2011-7* (see p. 57), a myriad of plotted points in grey, white and black, scans as data (of what?) recorded by some inhuman agency, for an unknown purpose, and this covertness in itself has emotional weight; only Ding's perpetually hand-applied facture keeps it in the human world, a world increasingly populated, as we know, by drones and self-driving cars and AIs in general, in which a progressively greater percentage of 'seeing' is done by computers. Many of Ding's more recent paintings, made on basswood, seem set either at night or in the black infinity of the digital, or both – relays from a bomber hovering over a foreign land, or incomprehensible streams of information. Of late the tones – though still rooted in the reds and greens that have run through his work – have begun to recall camouflage. Needless to say that this makes Ding's art timely, even three decades into his practice. The abiding marvel, of course – the sting of the work, even – is that he manages to achieve this replenishing relevance without fundamentally changing, only repurposing, the basic tool of his practice, that one iconographic symbol he began with: the printer's mark.

的。重点在于，丁乙的艺术允许（几乎可以说迫使）这些诠释存在。

我们看到，在这段时间，人类视觉转向了某种机器视觉。《十示 2011-7》（见第57页）由大量黑白灰色的投影点组成，看起来像是由某个非人类机构收集的数据（但是这些数据的内容是什么呢？），目的未知。这种隐秘性本身就有情感的力量。只是由于丁乙持之以恒的手绘技法，这幅作品才像是人类世界的产物。众所周知，当今世界有越来越多的无人机、无人驾驶汽车和人工智能；"观看"则越来越多的由电脑完成。丁乙的不少近作画在椴木板上，看起来像是夜景，或是身处无尽黑色的数字世界中，或者两者皆有（像轰炸机侦察外国时发送的信息，或是不可解读的信息流）。最近作品的色调（虽然还是基于一直以来使用的红色和绿色）开始让人想到迷彩色。毋庸置疑，这个变化让丁乙的作品和时代同步，就算他已经持续创作了三十年时间。当然，长期以来的奇妙之处（甚或是作品引人入胜之处）在于，他能不断地保持作品的相关性，却不需要从根本上改变（只需改造）他创作的基本工具，即他创作初始就使用的图示标志：印刷用的十字。

1 Ding Yi, quoted in 'From Performance to Abstraction: A Conversation with Ding Yi', 2015, www.post.at.moma.org/content_items/693-from-performance-to-abstraction-a-conversation-with-ding-yi
2 Ding Yi, quoted in 'Ding Yi and the Impossibility of Abstraction', Tony Godfrey, catalogue for Shanghart Singapore, 2011, www.shanghartsingapore.com/gallerysg/texts/id/3172
3 Tony Godfrey, in catalogue for Shanghart Singapore, 2011, www.shanghartsingapore.com/gallerysg/texts/id/3172
4 Ding Yi, quoted in 'Ding Yi and the Impossibility of Abstraction', Tony Godfrey, catalogue for Shanghart Singapore, 2011, www.shanghartsingapore.com/gallerysg/texts/id/3172
5 Ding Yi, quoted in 'Ding Yi: I Don't Know Whether This is a Golden Age', Goethe Institute China, 2015, www.goethe.de/ins/cn/en/kul/mag/20616719.html
6 ibid.
7 Ding Yi, quoted in Mary Beth Stock, 'Ivory Black: Ding Yi', *Art Asia Pacific*, May/June 2015, www.artasiapacific.com/Magazine/93/DingYi

1 丁乙，引自《从行为到抽象：访谈丁乙》，2015年，www.post.at.moma.org/content_items/693-from-performance-to-abstraction-a-conversation-with-ding-yi
2 丁乙，引自《丁乙和抽象的不可能性》，Tony Godfrey，香格纳新加坡画册，2011年，www.shanghartsingapore.com/gallerysg/texts/id/3172
3 Tony Godfrey，香格纳新加坡画册，2011年，www.shanghartsingapore.com/gallerysg/texts/id/3172
4 丁乙，引自《丁乙和抽象的不可能性》，Tony Godfrey，香格纳新加坡画册，2011年，www.shanghartsingapore.com/gallerysg/texts/id/3172
5 丁乙，引自《我不知道这是不是黄金时代》，歌德学院中国，2015年，www.goethe.de/ins/cn/en/kulmag/20616719.html
6 同上
7 丁乙，引自Mary Beth Stock：《象牙黑：丁乙》，*Art Asia Pacific*，2015年五月/六月刊，www.artasiapacific.com/Magazine/93/DingYi

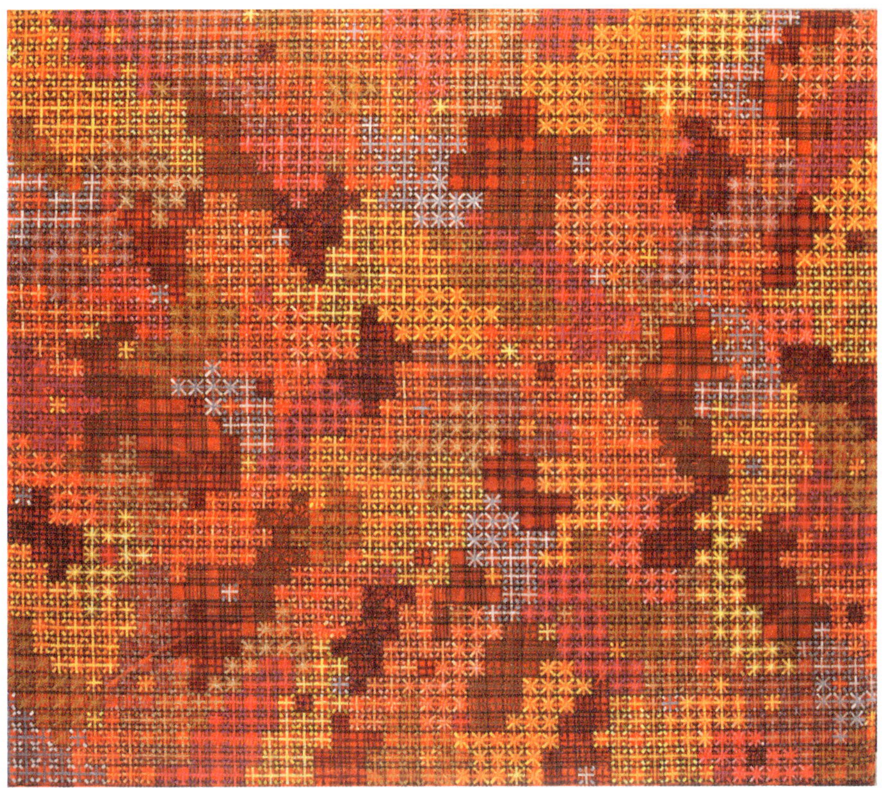

Appearance of Crosses 2003-9
(Scale 1:15)

十示 2003-9
(比例尺 1:15)

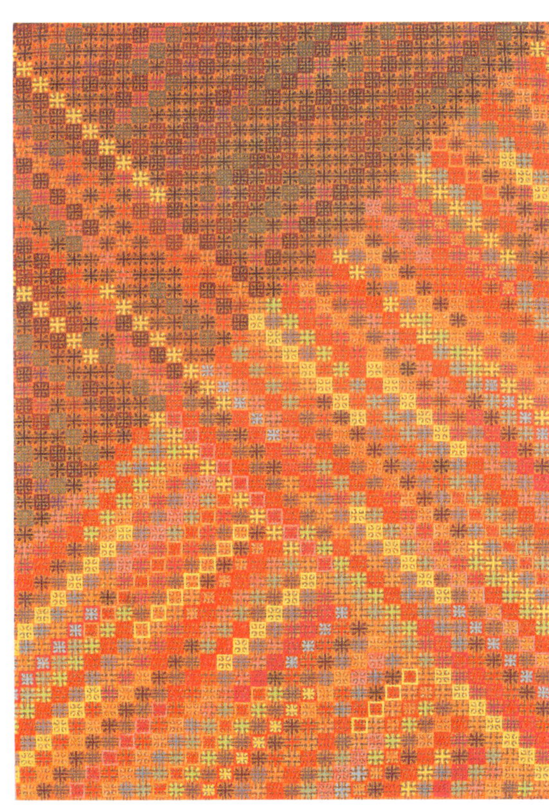

Appearance of Crosses 2008-2
(Scale 1:20)

十示 2008-2
(比例尺 1:20)

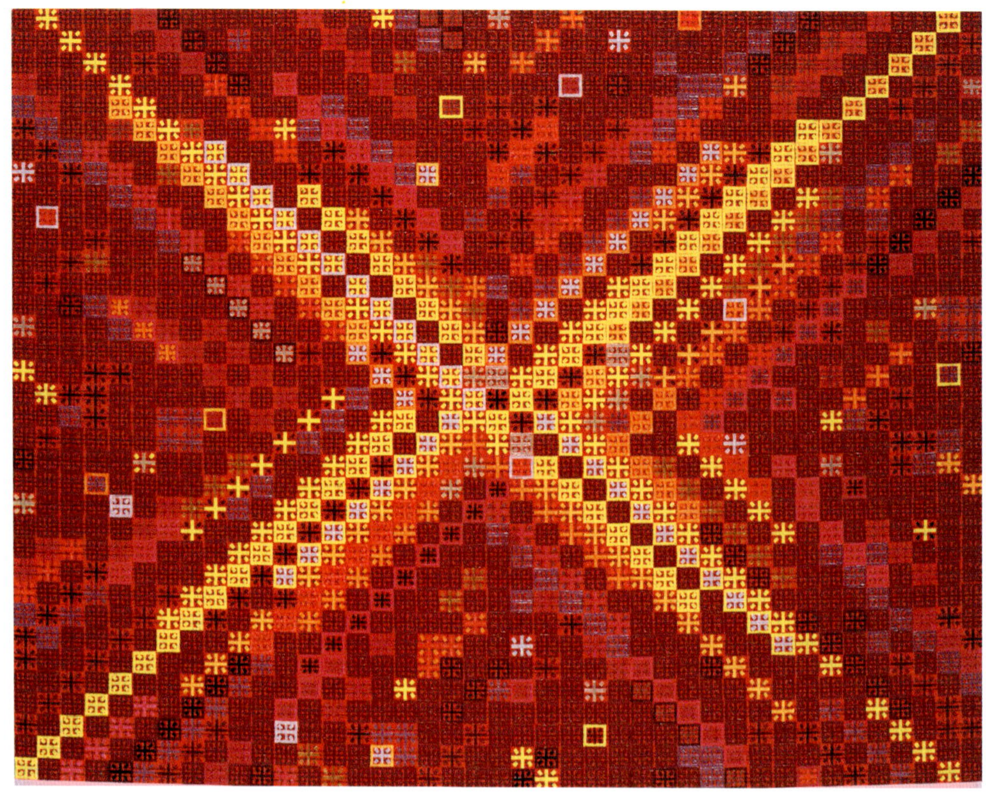

Appearance of Crosses 2010 - 2
(Scale 1:15)

十示 2010 - 2
(比例尺 1:15)

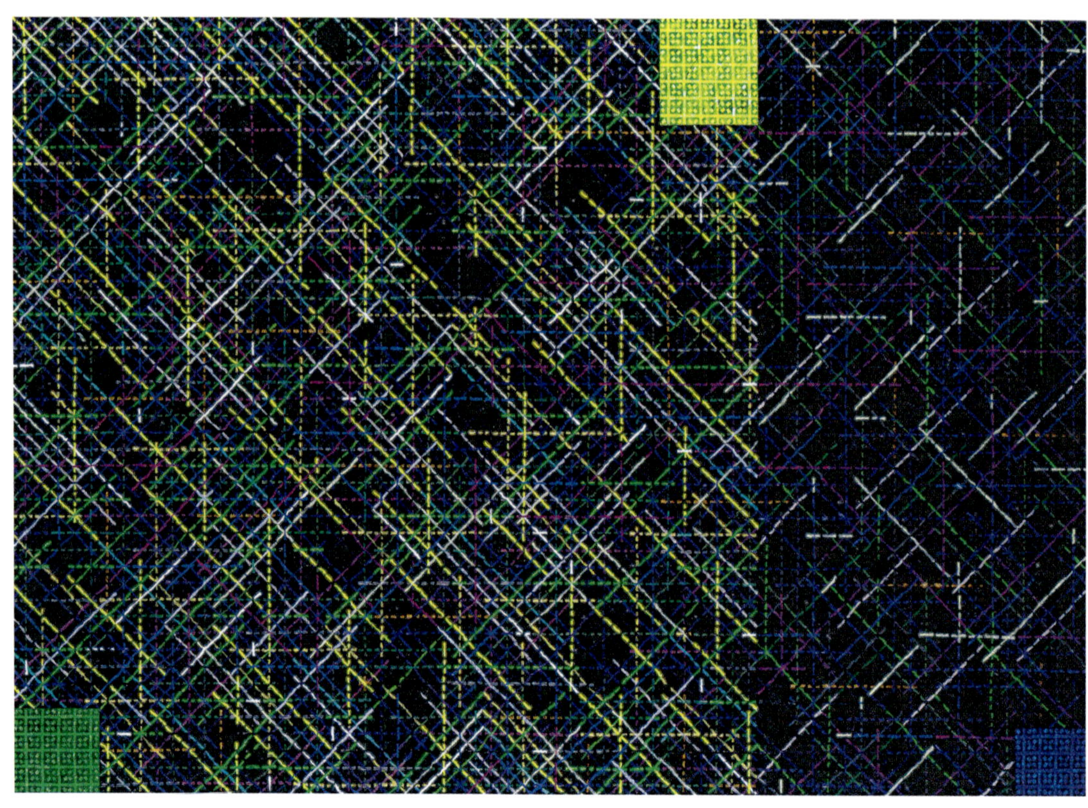

Appearance of Crosses 2010 - 16
(Scale 1:15)

十示 2010 - 16
(比例尺 1:15)

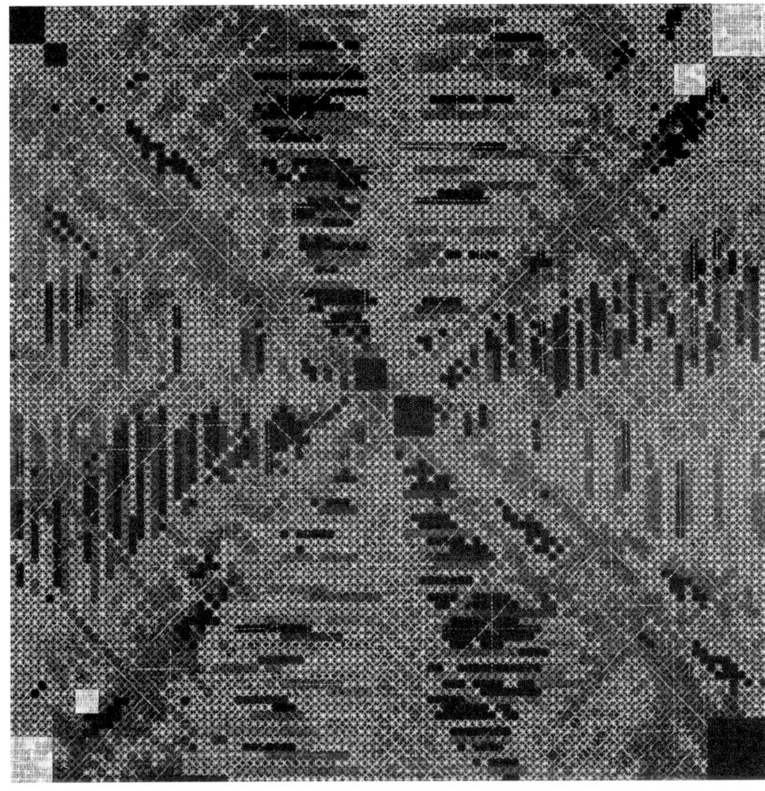

Appearance of Crosses 2011 - 7
(Scale 1:25)

十示 2011 - 7
(比例尺 1:25)

List of Works

作品列表

Cover
Appearance of Crosses
2016-5 (detail)
2016
Mixed media on basswood
240×240 cm / 94½×94½ in

封面
十示
2016-5（细节）
2016
椴木板上综合材料
240×240 cm / 94½×94½ in

1
Appearance of Crosses
2016-4
2016
Mixed media on basswood
240×240 cm / 94½×94½ in

1
十示
2016-4
2016
椴木板上综合材料
240×240 cm / 94½×94½ in

3
Appearance of Crosses
2016-5
2016
Mixed media on basswood
240×240 cm / 94½×94½ in

3
十示
2016-5
2016
椴木板上综合材料
240×240 cm / 94½×94½ in

5
Appearance of Crosses
2016-6
2016
Mixed media on basswood
240×240 cm / 94½×94½ in

5
十示
2016-6
2016
椴木板上综合材料
240×240 cm / 94½×94½ in

7
Appearance of Crosses
2016-7
2016
Mixed media on basswood
240×240 cm / 94½×94½ in

7
十示
2016-7
2016
椴木板上综合材料
240×240 cm / 94½×94½ in

9
Appearance of Crosses
2016-8
2016
Mixed media on basswood
240×240 cm / 94½×94½ in

9
十示
2016-8
2016
椴木板上综合材料
240×240 cm / 94½×94½ in

11
Appearance of Crosses
2016-9
2016
Mixed media on basswood
240×240 cm / 94½×94½ in

11
十示
2016-9
2016
椴木板上综合材料
240×240 cm / 94½×94½ in

13
Appearance of Crosses
2016-10
2016
Mixed media on basswood
240×240 cm / 94½×94½ in

13
十示
2016-10
2016
椴木板上综合材料
240×240 cm / 94½×94½ in

17
Appearance of Crosses
2016-4 (detail)
2016
Mixed media on basswood
240×240 cm / 94½×94½ in

19
Appearance of Crosses
2016-5 (detail)
2016
Mixed media on basswood
240×240 cm / 94½×94½ in

21
Appearance of Crosses
2016-6 (detail)
2016
Mixed media on basswood
240×240 cm / 94½×94½ in

23
Appearance of Crosses
2016-7 (detail)
2016
Mixed media on basswood
240×240 cm / 94½×94½ in

25
Appearance of Crosses
2016-8 (detail)
2016
Mixed media on basswood
240×240 cm / 94½×94½ in

27
Appearance of Crosses
2016-9 (detail)
2016
Mixed media on basswood
240×240 cm / 94½×94½ in

29
Appearance of Crosses
2016-10 (detail)
2016
Mixed media on basswood
240×240 cm / 94½×94½ in

35
Appearance of Crosses
1995-B13
1995
Chalk and charcoal on hand-made paper
39×53 cm / 15⅜×20⅞ in

17
十示
2016-4(细节)
2016
椴木板上综合材料
240×240 cm / 94½×94½ in

19
十示
2016-5(细节)
2016
椴木板上综合材料
240×240 cm / 94½×94½ in

21
十示
2016-6(细节)
2016
椴木板上综合材料
240×240 cm / 94½×94½ in

23
十示
2016-7(细节)
2016
椴木板上综合材料
240×240 cm / 94½×94½ in

25
十示
2016-8(细节)
2016
椴木板上综合材料
240×240 cm / 94½×94½ in

27
十示
2016-9(细节)
2016
椴木板上综合材料
240×240 cm / 94½×94½ in

29
十示
2016-10(细节)
2016
椴木板上综合材料
240×240 cm / 94½×94½ in

35
十示
1995-B13
1995
手工纸上粉笔,炭笔
39×53 cm / 15⅜×20⅞ in

35
Appearance of Crosses
1995-B21
1995
Chalk and charcoal on hand-made paper
38×54 cm / 15×21¼ in

37
Appearance of Crosses
1997-B21–1997-B24
1997
Chalk and charcoal on corrugated paper
260×80 cm / 102⅜×31½ in ×4 pieces

37
Appearance of Crosses
2000-8
2000
Acrylic on tartan
140×160 cm / 55⅛×63 in

39
Appearance of Crosses
2000-9
2000
Acrylic on tartan
135×200 cm / 53⅛×78¾ in

39
Appearance of Crosses
2008-21
2008
Acrylic on tartan
150×150 cm / 59×59 in ×3 pieces, 80×80 cm / 31½×31½ in×2 pieces

43
Taboo
1986
Oil on canvas
84×84 cm / 33⅛×33⅛ in

43
Draft 1987
1987
Acrylic on paper
23.5 x 21.5 cm / 9¼×8½ in

45
Appearance of Crosses
1989-7
1989
Acrylic on canvas
100×120 cm / 39⅜×47¼ in

35
十示
1995-B21
1995
手工纸上粉笔,炭笔
38×54 cm / 15×21¼ in

37
十示
1997-B21–1997-B24
1997
瓦楞纸纸上粉笔,炭笔
260×80 cm / 102⅜×31½ in ×4 pieces

37
十示
2000-8
2000
成品布上丙烯
140×160 cm / 55⅛×63 in

39
十示
2000-9
2000
成品布上丙烯
135×200 cm / 53⅛×78¾ in

39
十示
2008-21
2008
成品布上丙烯
150×150 cm / 59×59 in ×3 件, 80×80 cm / 31½×31½ in×2 件

43
禁忌
1986
布面油画
84×84 cm / 33⅛×33⅛ in

43
手稿 1987
1987
纸上丙烯
23.5 x 21.5 cm / 9¼×8½ in

45
十示
1989-7
1989
布面丙烯
100×120 cm / 39⅜×47¼ in

45
Appearance of Crosses
1990-5
1990
Acrylic on canvas
100 × 160 cm / 39⅜ × 63 in

47
Appearance of Crosses
1991-3
1991
Acrylic on canvas
140 × 180 cm / 55⅛ × 70⅞ in

47
Appearance of Crosses
1991-7
1991
Acrylic on canvas
140 × 170 cm / 55⅛ × 66⅞ in

49
Appearance of Crosses
1992-15
1992
Acrylic on canvas
140 × 160 cm / 55⅛ × 63 in

49
Appearance of Crosses
1992-20
1992
Acrylic on canvas
200 × 240 cm / 78¾ × 94½ in

51
Appearance of Crosses
1995-29
1996
Chalk and charcoal on linen
200 × 280 cm / 78¾ × 110¼ in
(200 × 140 cm / 78¾ × 55⅛
in × 2 pieces)

51
Appearance of Crosses
1997-4
1997
Acrylic on tartan
140 × 160 cm / 55⅛ × 63 in

45
十示
1990-5
1990
布面丙烯
100 × 160 cm / 39⅜ × 63 in

47
十示
1991-3
1991
布面丙烯
140 × 180 cm / 55⅛ × 70⅞ in

47
十示
1991-7
1991
布面丙烯
140 × 170 cm / 55⅛ × 66⅞ in

49
十示
1992-15
1992
布面丙烯
140 × 160 cm / 55⅛ × 63 in

49
十示
1992-20
1992
布面丙烯
200 × 240 cm / 78¾ × 94½ in

51
十示
1995-29
1996
亚麻布上粉笔, 炭笔
200 × 280 cm / 78¾ × 110¼ in
(200 × 140 cm / 78¾ × 55⅛
in × 2 件)

51
十示
1997-4
1997
成品布上丙烯
140 × 160 cm / 55⅛ × 63 in

53
Appearance of Crosses
2001-1
2001
Acrylic on tartan
140 × 160 cm / 55⅛ × 63 in

53
Appearance of Crosses
2002-2
2002
Acrylic on tartan
200 × 280 cm / 78¾ × 110¼ in

55
Appearance of Crosses
2003-9
2003
Acrylic on tartan
140 × 160 cm / 55⅛ × 63 in

55
Appearance of Crosses
2008-2
2008
Acrylic on tartan
200 × 140 cm / 78¾ × 55⅛ in

56
Appearance of Crosses
2010-2
2010
Acrylic on tartan
140 × 180 cm / 55⅛ × 70⅞ in

56
Appearance of Crosses
2010-16
2010
Acrylic on canvas
140 × 200 cm / 55⅛ × 78¾ in

57
Appearance of Crosses
2011-7
2011
Acrylic on canvas
300 × 300 cm / 118⅛ × 118⅛ in

53
十示
2001-1
2001
成品布上丙烯
140 × 160 cm / 55⅛ × 63 in

53
十示
2002-2
2002
成品布上丙烯
200 × 280 cm / 78¾ × 110¼ in

55
十示
2003-9
2003
成品布上丙烯
140 × 160 cm / 55⅛ × 63 in

55
十示
2008-2
2008
成品布上丙烯
200 × 140 cm / 78¾ × 55⅛ in

56
十示
2010-2
2010
成品布上丙烯
140 × 180 cm / 55⅛ × 70⅞ in

56
十示
2010-16
2010
布面丙烯
140 × 200 cm / 55⅛ × 78¾ in

57
十示
2011-7
2011
布面丙烯
300 × 300 cm / 118⅛ × 118⅛ in

Ding Yi
Published by Timothy Taylor on the occasion of the exhibition

Ding Yi,
18 May – 25 June 2017

Director of Exhibitions
Tania Doropoulos

Publication Director
Kate Wong

Design
OK-RM

Editor
Matt Price

Proofreader (English)
William Lambie

Translations to Chinese
Steven Huang

Printing
Amber Print, Latvia

Timothy Taylor
15 Carlos Place
London, W1K 2EX
timothytaylor.com

Distributed by
Cornerhouse Publications
cornerhousepublications.org

ISBN 978-0-9929309-9-8

Acknowledgements

Ding Yi and Timothy Taylor would like to thank the following people for their contributions and support in realizing this publication:

Richard Deal
Tania Doropoulos
Ariane Feng
Steven Huang
Oliver Knight
William Lambie
Rory McGrath
Seb McLauchlan
Vanessa Pike
Matt Price
Lada Sorokopud
Kate Wong

丁乙
本画册由Timothy Taylor 为展览

《丁乙》出版（展期2017年5月18日-6月25日）

展览主管
Tania Doropoulos

出版主管
王凯楣

设计
OK-RM

编辑
Matt Price

审校（英文）
William Lambie

英译中
黄一

印刷
Amber Print, 拉托维亚

Timothy Taylor
15 Carlos Place
London, W1K 2EX
timothytaylor.com

Cornerhouse Publications经销
cornerhousepublications.org

ISBN 978-0-9929309-9-8

致谢

丁乙和Timothy Taylor要感谢以下人士对于本画册的贡献和支持：

Richard Deal
Tania Doropoulos
丰静帆
黄一
Oliver Knight
William Lambie
Rory McGrath
Seb McLauchlan
Vanessa Pike
Matt Price
Lada Sorokopud
王凯楣

Timothy Taylor